Rethir
Reset Your Life

DECISIONS
THAT MATTER

FAY NIEWIADOMSKI

Decisions That Matter

First published in Great Britain in 2025 by
Candy Jar Books
136 Newport Rd
Cardiff
CF24 1DJ

ISBN: 978-1-918097-05-4

© Copyright Fay Niewiadomski

This book is dedicated to my children, for whom I would walk through fire, Jan, Zygmunt, Katarzyna and Anna Maria.

ACKNOWLEDGEMENTS

I would like to acknowledge my four children. These are the people for whom I would walk through fire: Jan, Zygmunt, Katarzyna and Anna Maria.

Without them, I may not have had the determination for many of the things I have done in my life. I have learned as much from them as I hope they have learned from me. My hope is that in turn my grandchildren will learn from their parents and help their parents to see the world through their eyes too.

I want to acknowledge the many teachers who never knew how much they contributed to my personal growth and development. Teachers leave a mark. Many of them underestimate the impact they can have on the lives they touch. Sometimes this impact is inspiring, and sometimes it is devastating.

The late Dr Irene Faffler ignited my passion for the theater and served as a mentor for the tens of plays I directed and produced.

Dr Charles Margerison and Dr Dick McCann of TMS (Team Management Systems) inspired me with their groundbreaking work on individual performance, team balance and work preferences in organizational design and productivity.

Stephen Walker of EBW Global taught me about business emotional intelligence and its irrefutable impact on effective individual, team, and organizational leadership.

Anthony Robbins and his life-changing Mastery University and Strategic Intervention Coaching programs are second to none.

I would also like to thank: T. Harv Eker and his Millionaire Mind and six-part Quantum Leap workshops; Blair Singer's advanced train-the-trainer program, Making the Stage; Joel Roberts on Impactful Communication; John Kehoe's Mind Power, Consciousness, and Manifestation programs; the late Tim Dew, unforgettable founder of GingerTech (now Immersive Edge); his amazing successor, Elton Daddow, commercial and training director, and CEO of Immersive Edge; and long-time CTO Niel Ballantyne, who now leads Immersive Edge, producing amazing business simulations for which we are delivery partners; Calvin Banyan of the Banyan Hypnosis Center with his 5-PATH® Hypnosis, Hypnotherapy, Master Hypnotist, and 7th Path Self-Hypnosis® Teacher certification programs; Bjørn Ekelund of Human Factor AS and Diversity Icebreaker®, designed to promote cooperation and peace through dialogue; and the husband-and-wife team who founded and managed GNOSIS Learning, Marinos and Anna Athanassiou.

Also worthy of mention is Mary Maloney, who brings out the best in people and helps them shine through her Revealing Genius™ workshops.

For the past five years, the VAB, my Virtual Advisory Board colleagues, have inspired and motivated me in more ways than I can count. I would like to make special mention of Mark Hamill, chairman and founder, and David Rodrigo Fernández Esquivel, co-founder and CEO.

I would be remiss if I did not acknowledge my writing coach, Mindy Gibbins-Klein, founder of the Book Midwife®. Mindy is methodical, thoughtful and competent. "The Book Midwife" is a very appropriate title, because it describes precisely and concisely what she does.

I have learned a lot from every single person with whom I have worked, whether or not their intention was to teach me something. These people know me and I know them. They include students, employees, colleagues, business partners, people I have coached, leaders in various sectors, as well as family and friends. I want you to know that every lesson I learned from you, whether easy to swallow or hard to digest, was valuable.

I have also learned a lot from the thousands of books I have read and the hundreds of great movies I have watched. As long as we are alive and conscious, we are learning. My dream is that my children, my grandchildren and my readers will themselves grow, learn and thrive in ways that will contribute to making the world a better place. By better, I mean wiser, kinder, more adaptable and open to learning – Humanization 5.0 and far beyond!

CONTENTS

INTRODUCTION

LIFE IS A CHOICE.
LIVING IS A DECISION.

WHY AM I WRITING THIS BOOK?

Have you ever asked yourself why family histories repeat themselves, or how you might learn from the past? You may have wondered how you might rethink, reimagine and reset your own life. In my view, this process begins with understanding past causes and responses. Such an understanding enables different decisions and different choices. Decisions and choices are central to asking ourselves what it is all about. Why all this effort and what do I really want?

I wish I could go back into the past and speak to my parents as an adult, to make sense of their experiences, learn from their wisdom and avoid their mistakes. When a fifty-year-old speaks to a fifteen-year-old there is a gap of thirty-five years, a gulf in experience, knowledge, contextual and situational awareness. I am not sure that the gap can be bridged, but I feel it is worth trying.

A personal record of life decisions and reflections may foster conscious awareness of the patterns that keep repeating themselves, both in family histories and human histories. If conscious awareness grows and blind spots are removed, the record would have accomplished a purpose: it would offer its reader the choice to do something different and better than simply repeating the mistakes of the past.

As time passes, our frames of reference may change so greatly that the reader no longer speaks the same language as the writer. Nevertheless, human beings are human beings. My book offers an opportunity to look back and extract past wisdom for present benefit. Human behavior and human experience can change through deep insights. The scenes change more quickly than the roles of the players. But roles can still be rewritten. The choice to rethink, reimagine and reset your role in life is always available to you.

WHAT IS THIS BOOK ABOUT?

The power of choice is the greatest resource available to us. Why? Choice enables us to do things differently when our first experiment fails. Choice is also the repository of resilience; it allows us to try again, and to apply our newly acquired knowledge, skills, experience and maturity to any challenge. Our need to find solutions to the many problems we face in life is the foundation of lifelong learning. Lifelong learning is a deep well of constantly renewable resources, and that deep well is itself the foundation for hope. There is always a better way or, at least, a different way.

But choices cannot themselves enable us to discover whether we are on the right path. Choice is a selection among alternatives. Chocolate or vanilla, which will it be? However, deciding whether we should have ice cream in the first place is an altogether different matter. That is a decision *of direction. Decisions require a longer view.*

In order to make important decisions, we should map cause and effect, action and possible reactions as far as possible in the chain of causality. When considering cause and effect, too often we think only in terms of the future. We should also consider the past. A backward chain of events helps us to identify root causes, while a forward chain of events enables us to consider possible consequences. Both understanding the past and anticipating the future enables us to make better decisions in the present.

But there are no guarantees. There will always be an element of risk. We have to learn to trust ourselves and have the courage to act based on the one constant we have. That constant is our identity, and that identity is profoundly shaped by our values. Knowing what really matters to us is the most important discovery of our lives. Start by discovering what your values really are. Then refer to your values on a conscious level when making important choices and decisions.

HOW CAN YOU BENEFIT FROM THIS BOOK?

In this book, I share personal stories in the hope that some of my experiences might provide valuable insights to my readers. I explore the difficulty of determining whether we are making decisions that are in full alignment with who we are. Are we really deciding, or are we defaulting to the easy option out of ignorance or convenience? And if we are, what does that really mean?

Do we have a pre-set life script, or do we create it during the journey of our life? Could there be such a thing as a unique vibrational signature for each of us humans? How does it work, and are we able to discern things about one another because of it?

I do not provide answers, but I do provide provocative questions.

If you are interested in getting the best out of yourself and doing things that are personally meaningful and fulfilling, my book is an invitation to take the time to focus on what matters to you. It is an opportunity to ask yourself questions about the direction and the outcomes you want. No one can give you prescriptions of what to do and where to go in order to fulfil your potential and achieve personal happiness. You are unique and therefore must be actively involved in this exploration. You must choose to be a willing partner in the design of your best life.

This book is not an easy read. You may even have to reread some paragraphs twice. Roll up your sleeves. This book may unpack more truth than you are ready for, but it will enable you to rethink, reimagine and reset your life on the trajectory towards fulfillment.

CHAPTER 1

A LACK OF COMPETENCE LEADS TO INJUSTICE

If you could choose just one superpower, what would it be? Would you want it to be expandable, adaptable and unlimited? Would you want it to be something no one could ever take away from you? What would it look and feel like and how would you share it with others if you could?

MY LOVE AFFAIR WITH LEARNING STARTED IN JAMAICA

How do we keep the flame of love alive and remain loyal to what we value most? How do we fiercely defend our humanity and our love for the things that make life worth living? It is neither through denial nor through surrender.

I was born in Lebanon and raised in Jamaica, where I lived for the first eighteen years of my life. It was in the sunny Caribbean that I developed a lifelong passion for learning. My insatiable curiosity about nature, science, aesthetics and many other areas of human development and growth lives on into the seventy-eighth year of my life.

My observation skills were shaped by nature walks to observe and document fauna and flora, and drawing with China ink the fine details I saw under my microscope. Amazing lab experiments, imaginative flower arrangements, exciting drama, boring sewing, creative cooking, competitive tennis and dreaded Latin lessons all added spice to my journeys of discovery.

By the time I left Jamaica to attend an American women's college in Lebanon, I had built up a large collection of seashells and butterflies all properly mounted, curated and labelled in Latin from phylum to variety. I gifted these to the biology lab at my school. Squandering all that work and knowledge was unthinkable.

My college years were horrible. There was such a huge gap between the quality of my school education and my college education. Added to this, there was the culture shock of returning to a country which my parents had left when I was a two-year-old. Their perceptions of Lebanon were based on a slice of life in 1948, and no longer held when I arrived to live and study there.

At eighteen, I did not have the financial means to go to a different college, nor the capability to acquire such means. But instead of becoming an educational casualty, I chose to make the most of the situation. Yet my undercurrent of unrelenting rebellion against the poor quality of the education provided for me never went away.

How could learning be subordinated to anything else? Making informed and responsible decisions requires knowledge, competence, objectivity and humility. We don't know everything. The audacity of thinking that we know best is outrageous to say the least.

The importance of a good education cannot be overestimated. How can a world worth living in be built upon a foundation of ignorance? What is the value of a decision based on a lack of knowledge, understanding and experience?

Just think for a moment. What does it mean when we ask people to vote? We are asking them to make informed decisions as adults. How can they do so when they are ill equipped to understand their realities? And what about the competence of the leaders who make decisions that impact the lives of tens, hundreds, thousands, millions, even billions?

LACK OF COMPETENCE LEADS TO INJUSTICE

Competence is the application of knowledge in productive and constructive ways. Lack of competence leads to injustice and abuse. When we do not know what we are doing but assume that we do, there is the potential to do harm, intentionally or otherwise.

On the other hand, applying what we know today does not mean that this will remain the most constructive way of doing things in the future. Learning is a lifelong responsibility, a skill that should be developed throughout our lives. Learning to learn and enjoying the experience is the most exciting and pleasurable process for remaining relevant and current.

INCOMPETENCE IS DANGEROUS

Incompetence is dangerous because it is based on ignorance. It is ignorance in action and it has the potential to inflict harm on ourselves and others. It doesn't take much to destroy a child's self-esteem and cause lifelong trauma. There was a time when teachers thought it was acceptable to put a Dunce Cap on a child's head. To add insult to injury, they would bring their victim to the front of the class and have a good laugh with the other children. Such incompetence remains prevalent today, only without the physical dunce cap. In time, many such victims become victimizers themselves, filled with hate. I have worked with many grownups who suffered the same humiliation in their personal and professional lives.

KNOWLEDGE AND COMPETENCE ARE NOT THE SAME

We often confuse competence with knowledge, but they are not the same thing.

Knowledge is about the information that we gather based on the period in which we live and the sources we have access to. Knowledge is also about the medium through which we acquire that knowledge – books, the press, community, culture, etc. Some studies have found that our thinking processes are affected by the type of media we are exposed to as we progress from childhood to adulthood. Reading is said to result in deeper, more complex thinking and broader imaginations. Social media, peppered with clickbait and short, slogan-like messages designed to keep eyeballs on screens, is believed to have the opposite effect.

Meanwhile, competence stems from knowledge, but it is always shaped and defined by external factors. How we apply our knowledge to dynamic external situations and to problem solving determines our competence. Knowledge itself is only one part of the equation. Knowledge is like a knife, sharp, dull or in between. Competence is our ability to use the knife to slice, dice or cause injury.

KNOWLEDGE IS NOT THE SAME AS FACTS

Facts are things that we can all agree on; they represent irrefutable realities. Knowledge is a mixture of beliefs, current information and siloed repositories of information about one area or discipline.

That means that knowledge and understanding are also very different things. How often do we question what we know? Consider whether or not your knowledge is current, reliable and free of inherent bias.

KNOWLEDGE AND EXPERIENCE ARE NOT THE SAME

What happens when knowledge is imparted by an authoritative source and further confirmed with certificates, diplomas and other 'legitimizers'? Is such knowledge always questioned as deeply as it might be?

The more we think we know, the greater the risk of confusing knowledge with competence. This reality check comes when we try to apply that knowledge. That is when we meet the complexity of a playing field filled with obstacles, opportunities, human behaviors and expectations. We discover that knowledge is not neutral, and understanding is not about facts. Rather, knowledge can be challenged and disputed by opposing bodies of knowledge.

I discovered the difference between knowledge and facts when my husband and I started a factory. Against all odds, my husband designed and produced high quality, low-cost extractor fans in Lebanon, which in the 1970s was an industrially underdeveloped country. We naively thought that having a great, high demand and affordable product was a winning ticket. Our naivete about local politics, ruthless competition and the impact of an impending civil war taught us some very harsh lessons.

That experience was bitter but beneficial, because we discovered how little we knew. We had overestimated the value of what we did know, and we had underestimated the devastating impact of the huge amount of knowledge, competence and experience we lacked.

THE LESS YOU KNOW...

The less knowledge we have, the more we think we know. We know so little that we are not even aware of how much we are missing. The arrogance of ignorance and the need for certainty form a wall of resistance to learning. Certainty is two-faced. We are so sure that we take a risk, or we are so sure that we don't.

The need for certainty is even more destructive to the development of human potential than the arrogance of some with a large field of knowledge. The less you know, and the stronger your need to be right, the greater the risk you present. Observe the child who still doesn't know that fire burns.

As a training program for salespersons, each of them with twenty-five to thirty years of experience, I once set up an auction sale of obsolete items. I asked, "Why don't you want to buy and use this iron that needs to be filled with live coals?" They had no answers to this question. They had not considered. They thought they knew it all already.

Part of the fun of the training program was to demonstrate how much they did not know. One of the challenges was to learn to dance the Macarena, itself a metaphor for resilience and adaptability!

LITTLE KNOWLEDGE IS A BARRIER

The academic David Kolb studied how people learn, breaking the process into four stages.

Stage One – Unconscious Incompetence: We don't know that we don't know and therefore overestimate our capabilities. Even worse, we are impervious to knowledge that is perceived as new or contradictory to what we think we do know.

Stage Two – Conscious Incompetence: We discover the fact that we don't know, and we now have the choice of becoming receptive to new information or skill acquisition. At this stage, we can go forward and learn, or we can deny the new knowledge. We might even seek to destroy the source of that knowledge because we see it as a threat to our need for certainty.

Stage Three – Conscious Competence: Here we demonstrate the conscious and willing acceptance of new knowledge and skills. However, we have to put in effort to develop these new understandings or skills. A lot of encouragement and a genuine desire to grow is required here; it is easy to rest on our laurels.

If the desire for and the perceived value of new knowledge and skills align with our self-concept, we can continue to move forward. Alternatively, we might make a U-turn and go back to our comfort zone and old habits.

Clarity of purpose is critical at this stage. Without intrinsic and extrinsic motivation, we may not form new habits and make them part of who we are.

Stage Four – Unconscious Competence: At this stage, the new habit has become part of both who we are and who we want to be. Skills can range from the relatively simple, like driving a car, all the way to complex sets of competencies such as those necessary for effective leadership.

The most important feature of this stage is that we 'forget' how we got to this new level. As a result, we might underestimate what it takes to get others to get to the same stage. We literally have to go back to stage one and reconstruct the pathway of how to progress to stage four. When that's clear, we need to design a method for transferring this knowledge and skill to others.

THE KNOWING-DOING GAP IS PROBLEMATIC

Closing the knowing-doing Gap is problematic. First, because we don't necessarily know *how* to do something. Second, because even if we once possessed such knowledge, it might have since become obsolete. We must keep our knowledge up to date. Most of us do not do so; it rarely seems like a priority among the pressures of survival and everyday life. Third, our competence can also become obsolete if we do not continuously put it into practice.

Moreover, because of Unconscious Competence, we can greatly underestimate the complexity of transferring knowledge, understanding and skills. Transferring partial capabilities is one thing, but transferring them at a level that enables another person to become truly competent is very challenging.

No matter how much documentation and detail is recorded, there are so many subtle behaviours and micro-actions involved in competence that it is practically impossible to transfer it to another person without an apprenticeship. One example is the case of repairing Braille typewriters, which are still used by many blind people in order to write. Yet master craftsmen can't find interested apprentices, and so the skill is being lost.

And this is only one example. What would happen if our communication systems were knocked out and we no longer had access to searches, AI and those other services to which we have surrendered our capabilities?

THERE IS NO USER'S MANUAL FOR HUMANIZATION

The knowing-doing gap is further complicated when we consider leadership behaviors that feed on the ignorance of others. The abuse of power, intentionally or otherwise, causes considerable harm. Abuse of power and influence is predicated on the decoupling of ethical behavior from the application of knowledge and competence. The ignorance of others becomes the fertile soil in which these abusers thrive. The application of knowledge and competence is a responsibility.

Using the influence derived from our leadership roles in areas where skill and competence are lacking is exceedingly dangerous.

Life is a long and interesting process of learning, unlearning and relearning. It can also be a miserable and systematic process of disconnection, disorientation and mental fading if we allow ourselves to stop learning.

HUNGER FOR POWER LEADS TO DEVASTATION

Consider the countless examples of the harm caused to millions by authority figures from so many disciplines and walks of life. Too often, religious leaders preach that we are good and they are bad. Meanwhile, politicians assume the mantle of judges of the greater good, and in so doing, justify death and destruction for their purposes. Business leaders, moreover, understand that ignorance is an economic resource, and manipulate "pain/pleasure" drives to enrich themselves.

How can we have a so-called democracy built on the manipulation of the improperly educated and ignorant masses? Masses who have been fully trained to respond to Pavlovian conditioning and masterful psyops? Thinking is really very hard work, and many leaders offer to relieve you of that burden. Just come along for the ride. It is fully automated.

CONVENIENCE IS A SLIPPERY SLOPE

Convenience allows us to receive reward without effort. We get that dopamine shot and go from one short burst of pleasure to the next. The pleasure ride is addictive and confusing. In addition, it leaves us begging to understand why we still haven't achieved happiness. Why not? We should be happy with the thousand pairs of shoes in our closet and the millions in our bank account.

Our preference for convenience and need for certainty act like a vice that keeps us in our comfort zones. Learning new things means failing and trying again and again, until we get it right; it means uncertainty and effort. Add to this mix the terror of rejection and of being unloved and unwanted. These fears are fully leveraged by fashion, cosmetics and many other industries, until every last cent on the credit card has been spent. The criticism and praise we heard as children is very sticky. It is hard to wash away or forget being called stupid, ugly or clumsy. These feelings stick because they were delivered with highly charged emotions by figures of authority: parents, teachers or others.

Wash your mouth, mother, and you too, father! Think about what you say to your children and, more importantly, how you act in front of them. What happens when you hurl hurtful words at them? The reverberations of those words never stop. The emotions they evoke form a bridge between childhood and our behavior as adults.

CONVENIENCE IS ALSO A TROJAN HORSE

Surrendering the disciplined and lifelong pursuit of knowledge and competence in favor of convenience and quick fixes is the Trojan Horse. It has infiltrated every facet of modern civilization. Discipline in the lifelong pursuit of knowledge and competence has been sacrificed on the altar of convenience. We have forgotten that learning can bring fulfilment; we think of it instead as the deprivation of pleasure. That is the destruction from within that the Trojan Horse has brought to us. Happiness and pleasure are not the same. Pleasure is fleeting, like the taste of a new flavor of ice cream, while happiness is a deep internal spring that feeds hope and optimism.

Discipline is not antithetical to happiness. It is the foundation of happiness. Many parents mistakenly believe that disciplining their children will deprive them of happiness and impair them in some way. Discipline is all about managing boundaries, both your own and others', and it is one of the best ways to teach respect. Discipline is not punishment. It is the exact opposite. It is about avoiding punishment when certain boundaries are broken.

PARENTING IS NOT JUST A BIOLOGICAL PROCESS

Parenting is not just a biological process; it is the foundation of social wellbeing and global stability. Where do we learn it and how do we evolve our skills as our families grow? Good parenting and good education must be constantly defined and reevaluated. Education that teaches every generation not only how to think but how to think critically and ask important questions is vital. In addition to thinking skills, education must be based on the skills of learning how to learn, especially in a fast-evolving environment.

The massive amounts of new knowledge, technological advances and the ever more powerful reach of communications that characterise the modern world make this imperative. We will not always be supported in our efforts. After all, critical thinking and continuous learning may not result in compliance and obedience. Often education and established social norms are out of phase with one another. As a result, this kind of education will by necessity question and hold accountable the religious, political and commercial structures of our society.

So what do we do? Do we dumb down education or do we get deeply involved in demanding the best education possible for the next generation?

Do we question the wisdom of giving our children false praise for things that they never really earned or achieved? Or do we destroy their self-esteem and self-confidence by imposing impossible standards and punishment? The answer is neither.

TIME SLOWS DOWN WHEN THERE IS DANGER

So what does all this mean? How do we solve problems that are within our control instead of whining about other people and things that we cannot directly change? We must remember that there is no situation in which we do not have the power of choice. Acceptance of things as they are is itself a choice, and one that we do not have to make.

Ignorance and convenience are very powerful and attractive alternatives to making a choice. Making a choice is hard. You need to learn, think, evaluate, consult and reflect before taking action.

My first son was born in peacetime, my second son in time for the start of a civil war; my first daughter was born in the corridor of a hospital as the bombs fell only meters away, and my youngest daughter was born by Caesarean section during a pause in the civil war. Out of such adversity came recognition and resilience, and it is these qualities that are required to make any choice.

Most of all, they are necessary to make decisions, which differ from choices in that they require a commitment and a long-term goal. I know how difficult it is to make such decisions, because I made one myself. My decision was this: in spite of the difficulties and the war and the threat of imminent death, I was going to live each day as if there was no tomorrow. I would do whatever it took to ensure that my children would be the best people they could be, no matter what!

And on that journey, I learned that making a definite choice is one of the most powerful things we can do.

STARTING A FAMILY IS A DECISION. HOW WE RAISE THEM IS A CHOICE.

With that recognition came many other realizations.

Problems need to be solved in practical ways, and that involves learning and doing. There is no room for excuses, otherwise your children starve.

Lifelong learning is a survival skill, and we should never compromise on that. Retirement is a death sentence – retirement killed my father many times over.

During the war, I nursed both my parents in the last days of their lives. My father had both legs amputated. He was a big man, but I found ways to lift him. My mother suffered from excruciatingly painful bone cancer, and I had to find the strength to administer regular shots of morphine. Experiences like these force you to recalibrate your priorities, optimize your time and make learning a daily imperative.

Choice is something that we confront thousands of times a day, because we live in a world that offers more options than we can possibly take advantage of. Choices are made in real time and continuously. The quality of our choices depends on who we are, what we know, how we feel and the situation we find ourselves in. It would be an impossibly hard thing to make conscious and intelligent choices all the time. That is why most of the choices are made for us by our unconscious and subconscious mind. Moreover, let's not forget that the slippery slopes of convenience are always available, and all too often we shrink from choices in favour of such conveniences.

AI IS THE OPIATE OF OUR TIMES

AI tempts us with ultimate convenience, unlimited sources of easy knowledge, and the surrender of our humanity to chatbots. What is our role as humans? Why have we bought into the myth that our value is fully depreciated and we should start to die at the prescribed retirement age? Neuroplasticity is a reality and lifelong learning is the most effective rejuvenator. So why do we surrender ourselves?

NOBODY WANTS CHILDREN ANYMORE

Why have birth rates gone down so dramatically in places where life has become industrialized, urbanized and pleasurized? Why are pets replacing children in our lives? What is our role as humans? The rarest type of human I have met are the ones who are at one and the same time intelligent and ethical. We need many more of this type of human if our world is not going to end through some form of mutually assured destruction.

The power of choice remains our first line of defense. Do not relinquish that power.

CHAPTER 2

LACK OF COURAGE LEADS TO VIOLENCE

We all have power until we give it away. We give it away because we don't know that we have it, or we believe power is a gift that can be revoked, or we exchange it to increase the power of someone else. This is how we put others in control of our lives.

NO, YOU AREN'T POWERLESS!

It is easy to relinquish our power. In some cases, we choose to do so. However, often we are oblivious to the fact that we have power in the first place. We always have power. We always have a choice.

Choices are not made in a vacuum. The emotional context in which choices are made directly impacts the outcome. Fear is the strongest of our primal emotions because it is linked to our survival. We need to live with it and tame it every day of our lives. Living without fear is impossible. So how do we learn to live with it and remain brave and sane?

First, let's explore some alternatives. We could surrender. We could destroy the object of our fear. Or we could tame our fear, look it in the eye and learn to decode the meaning to which it points. It takes courage to look fear in the eye. We need to cultivate that courage because, without it, life becomes colorless, flavorless and odorless.

LACK OF COURAGE LEADS TO VIOLENCE

Courage is a protective action driven by the fear of losing the things we value. It is a desire to protect and defend our values, principles and our concepts of "right" and "wrong". Violence is an aggressive reaction to the fear of losing our life, getting injured or losing material possessions.

Courage is a choice. It requires thought. But violence is only a reaction, an action taken without thought.

When we react violently to a perceived threat, we do not think of consequences but of the urgency of removing the threat. This kind of violence is about destroying the perceived threat before it destroys you. The greater the perceived threat, the greater the degree of violence.

Lack of courage leads to violence because, without courage, we miss our opportunities to choose, leaving us only the opportunity to react.

IS THE THREAT REAL OR IMAGINARY?

What we define as a "threat" is often only a mental construct, designed to motivate large numbers of people to act in ways they otherwise would not. This destructive behavior is driven by fear, hatred and anger that is cultivated and amplified in multiple ways. The purpose of doing so is to ensure the perceived threat becomes so imminent that there is an urgency to remove it. The closer and the more urgent our perception of the threat, the more extreme the violence exerted to remove it. And such violence is often followed by further violence, to confirm that the threat has been removed.

SHOOTING A DEAD SNAKE

I used to go hunting with one of my uncles and learned to shoot with a hunting rifle. I continued to hunt for a few years before giving it up entirely.

My parents had built a beautiful house with a garden. We had a small dog in the garden, and one day it came face to face with a 2.5-meter snake. Seeing this, I got my hunting rifle and shot the snake in the head. The neighbours heard the commotion and came to see what it was all about. Two of the men got their rifles and insisted on shooting the dead snake to make sure it was more dead than dead. Is this funny or crazy?

Maybe dark humor and dramas of the absurd are products of such displays of incongruous violence?

THE CYCLE OF THE MACABRE

Violence and destruction in response to fear lead to a macabre cycle of dehumanization and brutality. What are presented falsely as victory and power are in fact only manifestations of this cycle and serve only to fuel and replenish reservoirs of hatred and anger.

These reservoirs serve as the foundation for another cycle of this violence, repeated by unthinking generations. The new generation of destroyers either witnessed or heard of atrocities that their ancestors, parents, relatives and compatriots were subjected to. Their desire for revenge is the wick that sets off the next cycle of destruction.

COURAGE AND VIOLENCE ARE VERY DIFFERENT

Courage is a protective response designed to break the cycle of violence. Courage goes beyond self-preservation. It is based on something bigger than ourselves and our ideas. It is about the common good versus the "greater" good, which is itself predicated upon autocratic assumptions of superiority and exceptionalism.

Such exceptionalists believe that somehow they have the ability to judge, determine and put into motion actions that they and their followers decide are better for everyone. I was blown away when a warlord told me that he felt he was a god and that his followers just wanted to touch him. I fear that we live in a polytheistic world filled with replicas of this wonderful warlord. The question is who is crazier – the leader or their followers?

APPROACH THE GREATER GOOD WITH EXTREME CAUTION

The common good is a long-term view based on solving problems in sustainable ways. When the common good is served, all those involved receive benefits that are proportional, fair and based on deep understanding of causes and effects.

The greater good is based on winning and losing. There must be a winner and a loser. The winner must apply such overwhelming force that the loser is not only vanquished but preferably exterminated forever.

Humanity has succeeded many times in achieving both the common good and the greater good. We develop weapons that kill and maim. We also develop the medical expertise to examine corpses and treat the victims for whatever benefits can be gleaned. How ironic is that?

THE VALUE OF FEAR

My thoughts on this subject of courage and violence are not theoretical. I lived through a fifteen-year civil war in Lebanon that was a geopolitical balancing act, and I have experienced many other short-term conflicts both before and after. The region in which I live is like an active volcano that can erupt at any time. Eruption depends on the balance of powers. One power seeks to impose its vision of right versus wrong, of justice versus injustice, of victims and victimizers, according to its Machiavellian agenda. Other powers contest this according to their own.

Many years ago, during that civil war, I woke my children up at 5:30 am so they could get ready for school. We had all slept in the basement because that night the bombing was particularly intense. The children went off to school, and I got myself ready to go to my job at the university where I taught, packing a few documents into my briefcase.

When I arrived, there was no office. Smoke was still billowing out of the charred remains of the two upper floors. My office had been bombed, and seventeen years of dedicated work had been reduced to tangled metal, blobs of melted polyurethane, charred books, deformed picture frames and mountains of ash. All the work I had left to me was contained in my briefcase.

Those were the days when information had to be stored in filing cabinets. Columns and rows of filing cabinets going from the floor to the ceiling had been decimated. Now I had no office, no physical documents and nowhere to sit.

That day I had to ask myself some of the most difficult and life-changing questions: "Who am I?" and "What is my value?" Everything I had created over the past seventeen years had been turned into ash and charred debris. All that remained could fit in a small briefcase.

What I was left with were the memories of twelve-hour workdays, my children crying "Mommy don't go" and the years of living on four hours of sleep so I could get it all done. But in that moment of questioning who I was and what I was worth, I was able to define the true meaning of credibility and courage. I reminded myself that whatever was lost was something *I* had created, and therefore I could recreate it, even improve on it.

This experience fundamentally shaped who I have become: someone ready for any eventuality and fearless in being unashamedly myself.

Living with the constant possibility of dying or having your children's school blown up changes your perspective. It is like living frame by frame in a grotesque horror movie. In that movie strange things happen. Driving to collect your children from school, even though bombs are falling. Pushing away the muzzle of the gun and declaring, "I don't care who you are!" Sitting in a room with a young man who has been severely tortured and intends to shoot the professor standing in the way of his diploma and emigration.

Solving problems like these teaches you that courage, commitment and a degree of madness are necessary to successfully handle fear. Fear never goes away. Fear *can* never go away, because it is essential to our survival. Learning to master our fear, learning to work with our fear, is precisely how it keeps us alive.

FEAR IS BOTH OFFENSIVE AND DEFENSIVE

Fear is a defensive action driven by primal emotions of self-preservation or the avoidance of pain. Fear drives our responses, whether rational or irrational. Such reactive responses are based on the destruction of the perceived threat. When we feel as if we are backed into a corner, when we see no way of escape through dialogue or diplomacy, then violence becomes attractive. The greater the sense of desperation, the greater the degree of violence.

I am not denying the value of the "fight, flight, freeze or feign" instinct. But we must endeavor to be deliberate, as such responses can lead to unintended results.

WHAT HAPPENS WHEN WE FEIGN?

Accepting injustice and abuse at work by pretending that everything is fine empowers abusers. Sycophants who don't dare to say "no", even when they know their boss is dead wrong, do more harm to themselves in the long run. Abusers respect strength because that is what they most desire. They punish the weak and the cowardly because it is precisely this strength that they lack, and they justify the punishment by rationalizing that those sycophants didn't tell them the truth. This is beyond ironic. In their minds, dictators are never wrong or weak. It is their adoring followers who are so.

WHAT HAPPENS WHEN WE FREEZE?

The freeze response often occurs when subjected to verbal abuse. The freeze response enables the perpetrators of this abuse to keep people from advancing or receiving recognition for their work. I was once accused of being too bold and aggressive when I was the only woman on a committee of men. I responded, and that was shocking to the perpetrator, but they never made the accusation again.

WHAT HAPPENS WHEN WE FIGHT?

My response was to fight. Some colleagues preferred flight, only to see the same patterns repeat. Women are particularly vulnerable to abuse from authority figures, because of their socialization, education and upbringing.

Amanda suddenly lost her right to a promotion she had earned when she told her bosses she was ill. If she were a man, she could be ill and still be a president, but she couldn't do that as a woman.

Meanwhile, when Taline outperformed the peers in her market by a significant margin, she had to be kept in check lest she overestimate her contribution and value.

It is vital for women to have the courage to fight in intelligent and effective ways.

FEAR AND VIOLENCE GO TOGETHER

Because fear is ever present, so violence will likewise always be with us. Violence, physical or emotional, is a tool for the destruction of a perceived threat. Accordingly, the destruction violence wreaks can itself be physical, mental or emotional.

The timeline of violent reaction is usually short, and such urgency is driven by cowardice. Any awareness of consequences will be limited to the short term and not related to second-order effects. In fact, consideration of the line of causality will be non-existent. Fear drives short-term thinking, and violence stems from this limited view.

In times of extreme violence, gruesome things become normalized. Necklaces of the ears of those killed, or the heads of the persons decapitated, are displayed as badges of honor. Children, many children are subjected to sights like these. War is not a Hollywood production where violence and destruction are glamorized so long as those dying are the designated enemy.

Stop praising and applauding abuse and killing as strength. Abuse and killing are acts of cowardice.

ALTRUISM IS PART OF WHO WE ARE

Altruism is a tool for the preservation of the things we value even beyond our own safety. Altruism requires a long-term view and an understanding of second- and third-order consequences. When we understand the long line of causality, the chain of past, present and future events, things change. We appreciate the long-term consequences of destructive action. That understanding enables us to find the courage and the bravery necessary to preserve something of greater value than ourselves.

In all the work I have done with people who successfully and responsibly occupy positions of power, I have found that their deepest desire is to achieve something bigger than themselves. They want to find meaning and have impact on the world in ways that give purpose to their lives.

WHAT'S WORTH LIVING FOR?

Finding that positive purpose, and living it in spite of the cacophony of marketing and politics, the pressures of survival and responsibility, the influence of the untamed ego and the compulsion to preserve the trappings of success, is exceedingly difficult.

I found personal freedom when I truly, deeply and at the most profound level within my consciousness recognized that I do not need and do not want the approval of anyone. I have nothing to prove. I just want to be who I was born to be in every sense of the word. If some people don't like it, that is their problem.

When you feel it and believe it, not just say it, you will find that you have unshakeable inner strength. But it took too long for me to make this discovery. So how to accelerate this? What must we do to discover who we are meant to be as early as possible?

LEADERSHIP DEVELOPMENT STARTS AT BIRTH

Baboons are capable of war. If our ambition is to regress to baboonism, we are on the right track. But is that the best that humans are capable of? Great parenting and effective leadership are two essentials for the survival of our planet. We must parent and educate our future leaders, and we must do so more loudly than advertising and other such vacuous messaging.

Leadership improves the world around it. It teaches moral, accountable behavior in others. Once I dared to ask the big boss a big question.

Fay: "May I ask you a question?"

Boss: "Of course."

Fay: "When was the last time that you were absolutely wrong about anything?"

Boss: *Silence...*

That afternoon, several people called to tell me that they had been surprised to receive apologies from the boss regarding some past action.

My belief is that we must use the fight response more frequently and intelligently than we do.

YES, IT IS POSSIBLE!

I know it is possible to speak truth to power, to refuse tempting bribes and to bring people together in even the most extreme circumstances. I know because I have done so.

I once told the president of the university at which I was a dean that the curriculum they were looking to get endorsed by their highest religious authority had been copied without critical assessment. Moreover, it was totally misaligned with their declared vision, mission and values. There was an emergency meeting and the whole curriculum was revised by a competent group who were unwilling to take the path of silence and approve that which was unacceptable.

I told the president of a country to keep the big bag of money he was offering me. I told him that I did not need nor want it. By connecting the chain of causality and considering the long-term consequences, I realized that the money would only be a chain around my neck that could be yanked when needed.

And at the end of our civil war, I organized a nationwide, cross-confessional competition for excellence in English language teaching. Afterwards, I got the funding to send fifteen teachers from different communities to a summer teacher training program in the UK, where they could live, learn and appreciate each other as intelligent human beings.

HOW MUCH IS YOUR CREDIBILITY WORTH?

Several prominent political leaders who had pledged funding for the representatives from their region did not honor those pledges. I chose to pay a significant amount of money from my own pocket to cover the shortfall. My calculation was that the loss of credibility I would suffer from the competition collapsing would have been greater than the financial loss. *The Guardian Education Supplement* featured a full page on this program.

It takes courage and bravery to do what we all know should be done for the common good. This is one of the pillars of leadership development. Respect the intelligence of others by listening with the intention of understanding them. Interact and relate to them with kindness and compassion because you know that you are not the ultimate reference on the planet.

You are a lifelong learner like everyone else. Intelligence is inseparable from humility.

Imagine a world where we taught such values from kindergarten?

CHAPTER 3

A LACK OF COMPASSION LEADS TO CRUELTY

If you cannot feel compassion toward another human, you should seriously question your own humanity. Who are you? What are you capable of when you can inflict pain on yourself and on others without remorse? Do you dare to look into that mirror?

HUMILITY IS NOT SUBSERVIENCE

Humility is not about subservience or bowing down. Humility is about the awe we feel when we comprehend the vastness of time, space and the potential for discovery. Arrogance is diametrically opposed to this perspective of the world and our place in it. Arrogance diminishes us, while humility enriches us. The arrogant hold out the beggar's bowl while the humble see the unlimited potential for growth. The universe is rich with discoveries yet to be made, discoveries far beyond our wildest dreams.

THE ARROGANT FEAR LOSING THEIR IMAGINED SUPERIORITY

The humble see others as possible allies while the arrogant see others as threats to their imagined superiority. The arrogant have a point to prove: "I am better than you and therefore I give myself the right to subordinate everything and everyone to fulfil my desires." There is no room for compassion for others and no time to look in the mirror of self-awareness.

This lack of compassion leads to cruelty because it is based on the dehumanization of others, the lack of empathy and blind prejudice. It is a mindset based on the assumption that one human is superior to another and that, in some way, that superior human is endowed with the ability to determine the fate of other humans and their futures. The arrogant insanely claim that they and they alone know what must be done for the greater good.

What better expression of the "dark triad" is there? This lethal combination of narcissism, Machiavellianism and psychopathy. Such individuals have a deadly allure to those desperate for certainty and confirmation of their self-worth. The supreme irony is that these attractors are as psychologically damaged as their prey. The "protector" is as vulnerable as those who fall prey to them.

THE TOXIC ALLURE OF THE DARK TRIAD

There is no room for dialogue or friendship in such relationships. There is room for thousands of honeymoons though. As long as you show vocal and visible admiration, compliance, obedience and blind loyalty, the honeymoon lasts. That is, it lasts until you become boring. And it is inevitable that you *will* become boring, because you present no challenge. You are the echo in the echo chamber. That is when you are ditched for a new, younger, sexier edition or for a high-profile admirer that can be flaunted as the latest conquest.

There is no compassion either for self or others in these relationships. The narcissistic butterfly flits from flower to flower sucking out the nectar and moving on to the next colorful bloom.

THE ANATOMY OF COMPASSION

Sympathy, pity, charity and other similar emotions are too often confused with compassion. Compassion is based on a deep understanding of the perspectives, needs and feelings of others. This understanding is followed by an interest in contributing to better relations and the improvement of the wellbeing of those within our circle of influence. Pause for a moment and think of your circle of influence and how the size of that circle determines the impact you can have as a result of your decisions and actions.

APPEASE THE GODS OF FATE

Sympathy is ultimately about you. It stems from your sense of being in a better place than another. Pity is similar, a feeling generated through a comparison of your position with the position of another perceived to be at a disadvantage. Fear is the common root of sympathy and pity. These emotions are an unconscious affirmation of a sense of "superiority" and therefore personal safety.

Of course, sympathy and pity *can* compel charitable actions, but our motivation for these actions is to make us look and feel good. These actions may also be designed to avert the possibility of finding ourselves in similar positions of vulnerability as those to whom we extend our charity. Could our acts of charity be attempts to avert similar misfortunes in our own lives?

Compassion, on the other hand, begins with the expectations we have of ourselves. It is our way of dealing with ourselves when those expectations are not met. Put another way, compassion is how we deal with what we perceive as failure. Do we perceive failure as endemic and organic (i.e. we are flawed) or is it situational and reversible through better decisions and actions? In the case of the former, we are beyond repair, while in the case of the latter, we have agency through the power of choice.

WE AREN'T FATALLY FLAWED

We are capable of learning, growing and doing better. In a situation where we feel we are flawed, our emotional response can be complex. These feelings might range from self-victimization and helplessness to anger and a thirst for retribution. We lash out against our "bad luck" or "the poor hand" we have been dealt.

One of my children failed a school year and had to repeat the year. Another child decided that they didn't want to go to school at all. In the case of the former, I could have pulled some strings and made the promotion happen. In the case of the latter, I allowed them to stay home. Was I a cruel parent or was I enabling my children to take responsibility for their choices?

DO WE HAVE A LIFE SCRIPT?

Both these children excelled at their chosen paths. They achieved PhDs with high distinctions from the best universities on earth and built successful careers. They have mastered high-speed learning, and display inventiveness and application in multiple disciplines.

I did not try to prescribe remedies. How could I? We each have a life script that only we understand.

At fourteen I knew I wanted to be a neurosurgeon, and at seventy-eight I still want to be a neurosurgeon. The journey of my life has taken many twists and turns, but it has been and remains an incredible adventure of pain, joy, surprise and discovery. Yet one thing has remained constant: it has always resulted in new learnings and insights. As a result of all those twists and turns, I am now a fully qualified "non-invasive neurosurgeon".

That is what I do and want to continue to do until my last breath. It is not work; it is life affirming when I see transformation in the choices my clients make, the admiration of others in their circle. It is compelling when I read the messages of thanks I receive from them.

THE ROLES THAT ARE WRITTEN FOR US

My earliest memory (recovered through hypnotic regression) is the birth of my brother. I recall being in the yard outside my parents' home. I was playing in the dirt near an olive tree. I was wearing a pink dress with little patterns on it, and there was a very old lady taking care of me while the midwife attended to my mother. The joy and celebration at the birth of a boy was something that stuck with me.

I wonder how much these early memories resonated with me as I was growing up. As a little girl, I would hear things like "Too bad that you weren't born a boy. You are so smart and gifted." In my mind the sentence continued: "What a waste…"

So many other times I heard the soul-destroying refrain: "But you are a girl…" Or "Too bad that you're a girl. You would have done so much more if only you were a boy!"

I know I am not alone in this. Many of you have told me so, or I have discovered that it is so when we worked together. I don't blame anyone for the effects of hearing such things, because I too believed that crap for a long time.

NEVER FOLLOW PRESCRIPTIONS WITHOUT DIAGNOSES

The general wisdom/prescription when I was a teenager and a young adult was this: "You must get married and have children." I did get married and had four children. I also separated from my husband after twenty-three years of craziness and raised my four children mostly on my own. My mother was a pillar of strength and offered practical support until she passed away on Christmas Day 1988. I was forty-two.

I offered my mother care and love as she suffered from excruciatingly painful bone cancer. I will never forget the look in her eyes when she lost the ability to speak coherently, to form the words to express what she was feeling. I had to decipher as best I could. It is beyond heartbreaking to see a strong, intelligent and compassionate human being whom you love crumble before your eyes.

These things have shaped who I am and continue to become. Kindness and compassion are not signs of weakness but signs of strength. These feelings come from a deep well of humanity, deep insight and a profound understanding of the need to evolve into full humans. Such an evolution is vital for the preservation of the human race regardless of color and creed.

IF YOU ARE WILLING, YOU WILL BE REPLACED

Much of what humans do as work will be replaced by AI. But what about the work to earn our humanity?

As children, we can be very cruel, because the world is populated with just one person and that is us. It never occurs to us that we could be causing harm, because we are unable to see the world through eyes other than our own.

We should all find this deeply disturbing. Becoming an adult – a healthy adult – is learning to shed this myopia. But as our societies become more loveless, lonely and transactional, there will be no room for compassion – not even for ourselves.

CRUELTY IS ROOTED IN SELF-LOATHING

Cruelty is rooted in unconscious self-loathing and the projection of that loathing onto others in order to preserve our feelings of superiority. The output of cruelty is punishment and injury of the helpless, the unarmed and those who lack recourse to legal or other forms of protection. The inability of the victim to retaliate is an essential condition for the perpetrator. This is how perpetrators escape their fear. They spend their lives running from the fear of looking into their mirrors and seeing the depth of their cowardice.

Cruelty to the helpless, those tied and bound and gagged, unable to defend themselves, is one of the many manifestations of depravity. And now we have long-distance killing, the murder and maiming of millions with innovative modern technologies that take countless forms. Is that what humanity is meant to achieve? Is that what we want to leave as a legacy to future generations?

You can do better and so can I. What's stopping us? Is it that we confuse brutality with strength? Is it our belief that violence is the best defense? Or could it be that we never grew up, never learned to master our fears?

THE FRIGHTENED CHILD IS STILL WITH US

I pity those apparently powerful leaders. I have looked into their eyes when they think they are alone. I have seen who they become when the flash of media attention is over. I have seen the tiny, frightened little child inside, crying desperately not to be hurt.

These are some of the things I have experienced first-hand:

A billionaire prince who leaves his multiple phones to ring and ring and ring. By his own admission, he needs to hear the ringing to confirm how much he is needed by others.

A question put to me in all seriousness: "Would it be better to put quicklime on the bodies, to plough them into the ground and deny the massacre? Or should we make a PR statement?"

The rape of the maids and little girls brought in as servants by the husbands, and their use as warm bodies for sex-practice by their teenage boys. Then the violent beatings of their angry wives and sisters.

This is the damage wrought by the frightened child behind the eyes of the powerful.

THE DARK ABYSS

Abusive, degrading name-calling, the labelling of other humans, gives permission for cruelty. The selection of verbs such as "eradication" when referring to fellow humans is both pitiful and bone-chilling. What dark abyss of self-loathing and hatred must those words spring from? Remember, none of us are immune to this kind of violence.

We should never accept or turn away from the consequences of violence, because we too could find ourselves on the receiving end. We all have the power to make better choices regarding the kind of world we want to live in. Every dysfunctional and violent human being was born to someone. How did they get here?

BLACK AND WHITE THINKING IS INFANTILE

A world without compassion is a dangerous place not only for the prey but for the predators. The volcanic hatred and anger generated by atrocities only fuel further atrocities. Cruelty, even when amplified, cannot overcome hatred. Revenge will come even one hundred years later, because hatred is malignant and infectious.

But we are capable of compassion, and that compassion arises from our capacity to empathize with other humans. The desire to empathize starts with seeing others as equally human, and it opens the path to mutual understanding and problem solving. Empathy begins with caring for ourselves and valuing ourselves for who we are.

The black and white, judgemental world is antithetical to that. But change is possible if we can understand that a world based on fear and hatred is a world that will self-destruct. It makes no difference how amazing our modern technological advances are. We will simply use the latest and greatest of our weapons to destroy ourselves. That is what they are designed to do. Empathy is not one of the features on the designers' drawing boards, or part of the code in their algorithms.

EMPATHY IS THE ABILITY TO LOOK OUTWARD

Empathy is the ability to look outward, beyond our paradigm of reality. But the pursuit of empathy contains a trap: an outward look can take two paths. The wrong path is that of identification, the assumption that others want to be treated like you. This only encourages you to proceed with your autopilot programming.

The right path is to take genuine interest in who the other party really is. This requires a degree of intelligent vulnerability, an openness to the reality of the other.

When we approach other humans with genuine compassion they reveal themselves to us in ways that evoke compassion. Compassion is a path to inner peace, an opportunity to transcend hatred and fear. It takes courage to be vulnerable and to invite others to allow themselves to be vulnerable too.

THE BURDEN OF SHAME

Through empathy, we can enable others to put their burdens down and emerge with their self-esteem intact. I call this non-invasive neurosurgery; by practicing it, we can excise their secret shame. The chairman who lived with the secret of his deep attraction to another man for decades and struggled to keep the secret from his wife, children and colleagues; the doctor who forced her mother to abort her third child because she wanted to be the only daughter; the parents who practically extinguished their teenage son's self-confidence and self-worth by smothering him with "care" that was in truth only to assuage their own fears.

The catalyst for releasing such pain is lack of judgment and genuine compassion. These two qualities create the necessary environment of psychological safety. Prejudice and judgmentalism only perpetuate the suffering.

THE REIGN OF THE MONOPOLIGISTS

Prejudice destroys the fabric of what makes us human.

Feelings of inadequacy are the result of centuries of education and socialization that follow black-and-white formulae of right versus wrong. Add to this the "spiritual" psychopathy of various religious beliefs, and the distorting projections of political or military supremacy, and we discover that we are riven with the consequences of binary thinking. We are right and we will make you understand how right we are. You are wrong and you had better make sure that you understand how wrong you are. We are in control and you are not. Follow our rules, or else.

Our leaders are seen as strong because we confuse brutality with strength. We believe that strong leaders are the answer to all our fears. Why? Because they can protect us from the harm of "wrong" ways of thinking and being. Disappointment inevitably follows when we discover there is also an enemy within. That enemy is us. It is the destructive patterns of behavior that follow from our failure to comprehend what it is to be human, and to choose the courageous path.

PREDATORY LEADERS POSING AS PROTECTORS

The Dark Triad —narcissism, Machiavellianism and psychopathy – is precisely the profile of an inordinately high percentage of leaders worldwide. Followers select this type of leader because they perceive them as strong and able to protect them in the face of the enemy. They fail to see that the mask of the protector conceals the predator.

Such leaders have used the same tools of manipulation and control throughout history. These methods have been so successful in the short-term that they are now accepted as standard operating procedures and adopted in technology, marketing and many other fields.

The pathetic outcome of this type of leadership contributes to many harmful behaviors. Abusive parents and spouses are just a couple of examples.

Behavior is driven by our beliefs and emotions. How many times have you told yourself that you must be misjudging a particular person? And how many times have you absolved the hurtful behavior of others with your wishful thinking of how you would like them to be? We work hard to dismiss the inner dissonance between what we see, what we feel and what we want.

THE PROBLEM LIES WITHIN

Here are some examples that you may have experienced yourself:

The compulsive shopping of the woman who can't find anyone to love or be loved by. The deep disappointment on the faces of those who discover that you are not one of their co-religionists. The insatiable appetites of those who participate in the global plunder of the wealth of others, or inflict wars of subjugation to steal and control resources.

All this because humanity still has not discovered one simple truth: that there is never enough for those who feel that they are not enough.

So the savage desire for power through injustice, fear and the ever-escalating need for deterrence continues, because we cannot connect the dots.

In order to generate the compassion necessary to stop this, we must understand consequence beyond the first few steps in the chain of causality.

A good start would be to take our feeling of dissonance seriously. When things don't feel right, they probably are not. Stop and reflect on what is happening around and inside of you. Self-awareness, awareness of others and situational awareness are important areas of personal development. These capabilities help to keep us away from harmful relationships and situations.

SECURITY IS AN ILLUSION

From homes with security fences, windows with iron bars, security guards and attack dogs, to the slopes of a volcano of ever-repeating wars: such is the world I have lived in.

I worry that my children have inherited such a world. My intention was always for them to live in a better one.

Stop, tear yourself away from social media, from your grinding survival activities, and ask yourself, "Why are birth rates falling so dramatically in many developed countries?" Is it because we are building a more compassionate and just world?

What are you looking forward to this month? Is there anything beyond today or tomorrow that excites you and gets you out of bed at 5:00 am?

To improve the world we live in, we must attend to it. And to attend to it, we must first attend to ourselves.

CHAPTER 4

MAKING THE RIGHT DECISION IS HARD

Making decisions and choices is what our life is all about. Even if you surrender your will to others, you have made a decision. That decision is to become a dedicated victim of circumstances and subject to the whims of others.

CHOICES AND DECISIONS ARE NOT THE SAME

The time will come when you are faced with a decision that is hard but right. Choices and decisions are not the same thing. Decisions are strategic and signal a shift in direction and a change from dissonance to harmony with our values.

It can take a very long time before we discover who we truly are and who we want to be. It takes even longer to boldly embrace our identity. Life is a long journey of discovery, of steps and missteps.

We do not realize how many decisions are made for us. Many thousands of decisions are made on a subconscious level, our actions are simple and mimetic – this is what we have seen others do. Decisions are hard because they require the selection of a direction. The selection of that direction is fraught with opposing emotional forces. The need for comfort, security, love, acceptance and so on might all frustrate a decision. Confusions about what is right and wrong, and what the punishments and rewards might be, add further complexity. Decisions can feel like trying to see the way forward through muddy waters.

GETTING TO "I DON'T GIVE A F***!"

Decisions that are based on compliance and conformity are easier than those decisions that reflect our values and our true identity. Let's not delude ourselves. Such decisions are very hard, especially when we have a family, other dependents, a reputation and the expectations of multiple stakeholders. The consequences of our decisions can impact not only our lives, livelihoods and future opportunities, but those of others. It takes much more than time to get to the point where you can truly say "I don't give a F***!"

Our upbringing and family relationships have a profound influence on how our decision-making capabilities evolve. The social, economic, religious and environmental mixture into which we are born forms the substrate in which we go from infancy to adulthood. This substrate has a profound effect on how we see ourselves and who we believe ourselves to be. The direction of our lives depends not only on *our* decisions but on the decisions made for us by others in whose company we grow.

THE ANSWER ISN'T OBVIOUS

When we become more aware of our inner and outer worlds, the degree of harmony or dissonance between them can become challenging. Whose expectations do I meet, mine or theirs? Do I even know what I want? Do I even know who I am?

Finding answers to these questions means navigating a plethora of choices and conflicting emotional forces. Remember, a choice is not a decision. A decision can be compared to eating at home or going out to a restaurant for dinner. The decision is the direction we take. But choices, while less substantial, are more numerous; they are all the possibilities of what is available at home and the amount of effort we are prepared to put into making a meal; they are all the options available if we go out to eat, all the different restaurants and all the different options on the menu.

It is very easy to confuse choices with decisions because we don't distinguish between strategic and the tactical courses of action. Choices are easier because they are short-term and we can see the results immediately. There are very few dots to connect or consequences to anticipate. Strategic decisions are long term and more complex because we do not get immediate gratification. The outcome takes time and often requires adjustments as we navigate our way towards the desired result.

DECISIONS MEAN NO U-TURN!

We most fully experience the difference between a decision and a choice when we make life-changing decisions. Such decisions cannot be easily reversed and in many cases are totally irreversible because they set a direction where the only path you can take is forward.

Some of my own life changing decisions were based on convenience and misalignment with my values. One such decision was to pursue a degree in English literature instead of neurosurgery, which is what I really wanted to do. I was discouraged by the many real obstacles I faced, chief among them learning a new language, required to pass examinations and to practice in the country where I was living. I did not try to overcome these obstacles; I did not even begin to learn how I might do so.

Even though I excelled in English literature and communication arts, I always felt that I sold myself short. The misalignment of my decision with my values led to other poor decisions. However, when I turned down things like co-authoring research papers with my professor and a position and possible scholarship at Oxford University to pursue a PhD in Literature, I knew I didn't want to spend another three years studying English literature. It simply didn't feel like me.

DECISIONS ARE CALCULATED RISKS

But, I learned something from this experience, and when I was faced with other life-changing decisions, I made good use of this developed understanding. I didn't want to go down the easy path of convenience ever again.

My most difficult decision involved separating from an alcoholic and abusive husband and taking on full responsibility for raising four children.

Almost as difficult was my decision to resign from a deanship and a secure job-for-life in favor of self-employment. I made that decision knowing that I had very little in my bank account. And as I built my business, I repeatedly refused to get sucked into political roles, in spite of the incentives and "comfortable rewards".

Two convictions became guidelines for my decisions. The first was this: failure was not an option. I knew that I had the competence and intellectual resources to do what I had committed to do. And second: I would never surrender my independence or compromise my values for anyone. I would find an intelligent way forward by determining how best to navigate through the many obstacles that are a part of a life well lived.

No wonder we are confused. In this journey we call our lives, it takes a lot of losses and gains to figure out what we really want. Most importantly of all, it takes time to uncover our non-negotiable priorities and values. There are millions of "menus" presented to us every day, and they are filled with many subtle and not so subtle temptations, pressures and even coercions.

We are still in the jungle, only today it is not green, and the threats come from our fellow humans.

VALUES DRIVE DECISIONS

We are assaulted daily by media of all types, not to mention the social pressures of family life, work and other responsibilities. We literally do not have the time to see ourselves or take the time to think. It is unrelenting programming designed to leverage our need for love and acceptance.

It leaves us ignorant, and our willing acceptance of ignorance of the facts in exchange for certainty and a sense of belonging is absolutely brutal.

Are you in the right box? Which club do you belong to? The Brand Club, the Fan Club, the Fad Club, the Am I Doing the Right Thing Club?

How confusing, to the young and the old, the sick and the stable, those with direction and those without direction alike. Are you confused? If you aren't, you are a unicorn!

It takes a strong awareness of our values, and the determination to adhere to them, to maintain fixity of purpose. Values are what we cherish most and will not compromise. Values are a core component of our identity, and consistency with our identity is the most powerful driver of our behavior. Values can be positive and constructive or destructive and dangerous.

How do we uncover our values and get to understand how they impact the course of our life's journey? Consider the most difficult decisions you have ever made in your life and ask yourself what was the nature of the inner conflict you were trying to resolve. By dissecting those difficult decisions, you will not only uncover your non-negotiable values but identify the significant turning points in the direction your life journey took.

TAKING INVENTORY OF DIFFICULT DECISIONS

Here is a more detailed description of my own value-driven decisions.

After devoting seventeen years of my life to setting up a school and a university, serving in many senior leadership positions that culminated with a deanship, I finally resigned. This decision took three years – three years of inner battle with myself. It meant the pressures of self-employment, forgoing free tuition for my children at the university, and dealing with social stigma, the false assumptions of those who couldn't imagine anyone walking away from such a "wonderful" and lucrative position.

Refusing to accept bundles of money from a top politician, writing the figure I wanted on a blank check in order to give a "pass" to someone unqualified, specifying the salary and the benefits I wanted in order to withdraw my resignation... My answer was "No!" to all these things.

The power of that "no" represents independence to me. I knew without any doubt that I did not want to be beholden or blackmailed.

IT IS ALL IN THE DISQUALIFICATIONS

Refusing political roles was easy. Such positions involved things way outside of my value system. I have identified three key "qualifications" of those who get into positions of what they think of as power: a) that they are, in truth, unqualified for the position; b) that they are in some way compromised and thus easily controlled; and c) that they desire compensation above all and are therefore blindly loyal because they would never be able to "earn" an equivalent income solely due to their capabilities.

VALUES CAN BE LETHAL, SO?

It is difficult, at times even life-threatening, to stay true to our values. The first cohort of students enrolled in the communication arts program at my university were denied their diplomas. The objective was to force them to move to a different university. There was no academic or legitimate financial reason for denying their diplomas. I was responsible for those students and refused to accept the coercion. I created a legal file with all the supporting documents and sent it by courier to all the members of the university board. I made sure to personally hand a copy of that file to the VP who was responsible for this illegal action.

A week later, while I was driving my old Range Rover on the highway, this same VP tried to push me off the road. I had the presence of mind and bravado to push his car back. We both survived what could have been a fatal incident. The subject was never spoken of, but when we next met, at the sight of me his complexion grew several shades lighter.

ASSERTIVENESS IS MEASURED; AGGRESSION IS BLIND

Later, I assumed a consulting role for a leading bank. The CEO attempted to break my contract using false claims of incompetence. He refused to implement the arbitration clause in our contract, which would have required bringing in experts to determine whether or not there had been any failure to fulfil the terms of our agreement. He and his team used various methods of intimidation and humiliation to force me to drop my claims for compensation.

These methods varied: one day, this CEO claimed that he hadn't asked me to leave, yet when I arrived at my office, I found it closed. Another tactic was intimidation, an offer to move to an office in a secluded garage near to the security guards under his control. When I said I would accept, this was the last straw for him.

The final outcome was a proper settlement and payment of my dues. Was I lucky? No, I refused to cave in. I employed the weapons that were available to me and that accorded with my values: transparency, the open invitation to use expert scrutiny, making sure I was accompanied by witnesses in all my conversations, and I also strategized with a prominent lawyer. Wisdom and assertiveness, not blind aggression, contributed to the positive outcome.

Selling out our values is soul crushing; living by our values is elevating. Make sure that you surround yourself with people who share your values, because it will help you live by them yourself.

If you have a family, your values will be mirrored, for better or for worse. Those same values will become part of your family culture and get transmitted from generation to generation. Make sure that your values are what you really want them to be, because they will determine the depth and breadth of not only your dreams, but those of your circle.

Are you someone your circle wants to be like, or are you someone they want to be the exact opposite of?

CHAPTER 5

PERFECTION IS NOT A GOAL. IT IS AN IMPOSSIBLE STANDARD

When we set impossible standards for ourselves and others, does it mean that we have incredible amounts of ambition, or are we simply providing ourselves with the ultimate excuse for falling short?

PERFECTIONISM IS A DISEASE

Aspiring to ambitious standards is the path to success. Take a moment to consider that statement. "Ambitious" means "achievable"; it does not mean setting impossibly high standards. It does not mean the futile pursuit of perfection. Who in their right mind would agree to run a race in which the rules kept changing, and the finish line kept moving further and further away? So why do so many of us do exactly that?

Perfectionism is a disease that many of us have been infected with. Others have been subjected to living with people who themselves are afflicted with the disease. When I say "Perfection is a disease" many of those suffering from it are offended. So many proudly describe themselves as "perfectionists". I was once one of them. I laugh out loud when I listen to the trite advice of those who say "When asked about your weaknesses, tell them perfectionism." There is an irony to this, but not that which is intended; perfectionism really is a weakness!

WHO DECIDES PERFECTION?

Who is in charge of determining what is perfect? Who gives the pass/fail score? When do we know that we have achieved the impossible? These questions penetrate to the root cause of the disease, because when striving for perfection, the only score we can ever achieve is "fail".

Pursuing perfection, we are no more than that little hamster running on the wheel to nowhere. Inevitably, we will not only discover that what we have produced is imperfect; we will also discover that we don't know what perfect is.

If we use comparison with others as a basis to determine perfection, we will only ever realize that someone else has surpassed us. How healthy is it to discover, over and over again, that when you think you have reached the finish line, you have in reality fallen short?

We have to be mad or stupid to continue on the path to perfection. It is the same as the path to nowhere.

WHO IS THE DECIDER?

When we have the disease of perfectionism, we are not in control, because we are not the ones who set the standards we are trying to achieve. We have literally put someone or something else in control of our lives. When you are not in control of your own standard, you will always hold the losing hand.

It should not come as a surprise that fear of failure is one of the principal consequences of perfectionism. And what if that inevitable failure is reinforced with severe punishment, from an abusive parent, teacher, boss or god?

I have seen the impact of that on myself and on my four children, and I observed in the most painful way the defensive strategies we each developed in order to survive or escape punishment.

POSTPONE, KEEP A LOW PROFILE AND DISENGAGE

Here are some of our survival strategies: procrastination, keeping a low profile, and emotional disengagement. We put off doing things as long as possible because the risk of failure, and the prospect of punishment haunts us. The soul-crushing emotions of fear and guilt lead us to disengage emotionally, and the impossibility of succeeding makes this disengagement first habitual, then reflexive.

To avoid scrutiny, to escape punishment, we keep a low profile, impacting relationships and resulting in the selection of "broken" people as friends.

So easily, so profoundly, are our lives derailed by the pursuit of something we can never reach.

CONFRONTATION AND HYPERVIGILANCE

The justification for much brutality is that it ensures a child behaves in line with the definition of perfection set by a self-loathing and mentally ill parent.

The result is that, to avoid rare moments of lucidity, the punisher must dull any recognition of wrongdoing with self-punishment and alcohol. Meanwhile the punished develop ways of hiding to escape punishment. Some of these include out-learning and outperforming the punisher, becoming expert in multiple fields that serve the purpose of survival, such as hypervigilance and deep distrust of others.

All these survival mechanisms are further underscored by the need for reassurance, approval and praise. The punished often seek the company of a safe second-party. This is to maintain a sense of safety, ensuring that the results of any achievement are never the sole responsibility of the doer until the final outcome is assured. Then if the result is successful, it can be declared publicly and praise received.

THE POPULARITY CONTEST

Sometimes children are singled out as the favorite. Such children are conditioned to need to be the best in order to remain in the good graces of the punisher. This puts them in opposition to their siblings, and their lives become popularity contests. These children learn to say, "It is not my fault! It is them that need to be punished, not me!"

What a toll that takes. The child struggles not only with the fear of punishment but the guilt of causing others to be punished. Some of the consequences of such a childhood are permissiveness towards others, overreaction to perceived criticism, the need for public acknowledgement and praise, and the selection of partners and friends who are in some ways weak or inferior by comparison.

THE PROTECTIVE CLOAK OF INVISIBILITY

To avoid punishment, other children seek to become invisible. Strategies for maintaining invisibility include caution, attention to detail and sensitive antennae to the outside world . Discipline in how things need to be done, and careful consideration before action are hallmarks of such children. They often grow to achieve excellence in areas and disciplines where there is a high level of predictability and control. The downside is the negative impact on their human relationships. They rely overly on logic versus warm emotional expression and vulnerability, and they are often highly stressed in social settings and networking events. Invisibility impacts both self-esteem and self-confidence and, as a result, can limit opportunities in life.

GOOD WILL BE REWARDED IS BS!

Life is not fair or just and never will be. How could life be fair? We do not control natural events or the incredibly complex web of human relationships that surround us. Nevertheless, the myth that good will be rewarded lives on.

Building false hope of reward could be a survival mechanism. Perhaps that is why so many believe they will not be rewarded until after death. No one will ever know whether this is true or false, and so the mechanism is protected.

But in truth such a belief is only crippling. It succors

those who give up, those who blame others, and those who set themselves up as the judges. All your suffering and all your good deeds will be computed in the cosmological mathematical calculation, and you will eventually be rewarded or punished. How perverse!

It is essential that we stop this crazy belief that some mythical perfection will simply manifest itself, as a reward for all our trials. Let's focus instead on how to make life better and kinder and how to take responsibility for doing so – how to evolve into the higher quality of human beings we claim to be.

GENIUSES ARE MISTAKEN FOR FOOLS BY FOOLS

We are all able to cite examples of times we have seen that life is not fair. We can also find moments when things went in our favor. But those of us who grow up with the idea that we are capable of doing and learning throughout our lives encounter the latter more frequently. This is no coincidence.

When we encourage others without patronizing their intelligence and lavishing false praise on them, we equip them to create such moments. Each of us is exceptional at something. Stop comparing and diminishing your children, your employees and others whose lives you impact. Help them to discover who they are and how they can become the best version of themselves.

It is worth reflecting on the astonishing achievements of Antoni Gaudí. It has been more than 100 years since he died, and his imagination still drives the ongoing construction of the Sagrada Família Basilica, a breathtaking achievement of art and architecture. But all his achievements began with a nurturing parent.

As a child, Gaudí was too ill to play outside. So his devoted mother Antònia Cornet placed his bed next to a large window with a view of the family gardens. The garden's curved lines, twisting shapes and rich colors captured Gaudí's imagination. He loved how every blade, leaf and flower was so beautiful and unique. And later in life, this deep fascination with nature's forms inspired his architectural designs.

No one knew who Gaudí was when, in his last hours, he was hit by a tram. He was mistaken for a poor and insignificant person and so passersby did not bother to help him. A policeman finally obliged a taxi driver to take him to a hospital. There someone recognized him, but it was too late. Those who wondered whether he was a fool or a genius can find their answer in the Sagrada Família Basilica.

POLITICAL CORRECTNESS OR SILENCE?

It took my idealistic self many years to understand that remaining politically correct brought many more material rewards than genuine achievements. I saw sabbatical leaves and scholarships being handed out to those who had done far less than I had. It took time for me to understand why they were chosen over me.

I also recognized that I would not value such awards and recognitions unless they were based on factual achievements. Achievements which I considered worthy. I would not pay to have my photo on the front of a magazine or an article written about me. The issue is not the payment. It is the falseness of empty achievements.

The greatest gifts we can give our children or those entrusted into our care are self-reliance and self-confidence.

Such are the foundations of true self-esteem – not the fripperies of false rewards.

We must change the rules of the game for the next generation. We must teach them to think strategically, and to look at the big picture as well as the details. We must nurture their curiosity, encourage them to ask uncomfortable questions, think critically and develop the habit of investigation. It is a sad world where the size of your ass becomes the barometer of success. It is even sadder when there is such a proliferation of role models that look like they have been punched out of a high-volume production line in a fully robotized factory. Is our aim humanization or baboonization?

WE DO NOT NEED PERMISSION

We do not need permission from anyone to develop ourselves and those whose lives we impact. We must encourage both ourselves and others to engage in the world around us through unending learning and growth. The alternatives are vegetating in front of the TV; sitting alone, mesmerized by social media; seeking false popularity or shopping for self-esteem.

I have felt the most profound pleasure, the deepest sense of achievement, only when seeing the transformation in the lives of those I have touched and empowered. Self-confidence, self-esteem and solid, repeatable capabilities – these are the true rewards.

My own children have been my greatest inspiration, my proudest examples of how you can be lifted out of despair and realize that everything is possible. If you see life as a never-ending journey of growth and learning, you can do anything.

We have self-renewing and self-updating software in our brains. The journey doesn't end until the very last breath of life leaves us.

WHOSE LIFE HAVE YOU TOUCHED?

Someone once wanted to interview me before deciding whether or not to have me as their coach. "Tell me about your children," they asked. My answer was and will always be that my children are the greatest achievement of my life. In spite of a fifteen-year civil war, in spite of changing schools and countries, in spite of a truly challenging childhood, today they each stand head and shoulders above many. And not because they or I am arrogant, but because they combine two of the rarest qualities among humans – competence and decency.

WHAT IS LEADERSHIP ANYWAY?

My definition of leadership is this: a chemistry that combines competence, courage and compassion. This conviction comes from my life experience and my personal and professional exposure to what seemed like insurmountable challenges. I have worked with many different industries and visited many dangerous places, interacted and cooperated with all shapes, colors and forms of humanity. Global citizenship is earned. It is not a slogan but a reality – one that I created for myself.

My fascination with the workings of the human brain has never faded away. Today I not only describe myself as a non-invasive neurosurgeon, but I fully embrace, metaphorically at least, the skillset that goes with it. When I work with a person in a coaching relationship, I feel as if there is literally an invisible bridge between my mind and theirs. Without the need for words, I touch the parts of their lives that need healing, and they ask in astonishment ,"How did you know?"

I am not sure I have the answer. I simply allow myself to become a receiver; my ego recedes far into the background and my focus is fully on my client. At the end of each session, I feel truly exhausted, but I am re-energized when I know that their lives have changed for the better.

The question is always the same: how can we be sure that we have found and embraced our true identity?

CHAPTER 6

COMPETENCE IS GENDERLESS

When are we going to face up to the fact that we are all *people? We are all subject to the normal distribution curve, regardless of gender. When it comes to competence, some will be exceptional, either in a positive or in a negative way. The majority will be in the middle – neither brilliant nor dull, just okay.*

EVERY GENERATION CALLS ITS IGNORANCE TRUTH

Finding our true identity requires that we weed out the confusing and corrupting information that has been stuffed into our heads. We are steeped in the current ignorance of their times. Today what we congratulate ourselves on is simply the modern brand of ignorance. Future generations will look at our "truth" and wonder how we got to those conclusions.

Let's begin with competence. Competence is genderless unless we choose to make it otherwise. Just as there are stupid women, there are stupid men. We all have different levels of perceived intelligence and none of these levels have anything to do with gender.

The only relevance of gender to intelligence is when our hormones intervene. I bet, if you are honest with yourself, you can make a long list of things you wouldn't have done if you had thought about them before mindlessly reacting to the upheaval in your blood chemistry. Right?

WHY? WHY? WHY?

I have always wondered why it is that we don't see men and women as equals. Society has expended countless generations educating, socializing, conditioning and inculcating the belief that men are superior to women. Men and women are different and each contribute in their own way to the development of humanity. Why does difference morph into hierarchies of superiority versus inferiority? Why not view our differences as complementary and necessary for a balanced partnership in the development of healthy families and societies?

The answer is not very difficult to find. Consider all the stories we are told and the roles boys and girls play in those stories. When it comes to the roles assigned to men and women, for me there is no difference between fairy tales and religious education. These same roles have been assimilated into the biases and attributes assigned to men and women in our lives today. They are visible in the statistical distribution of leadership roles in business, science and politics. They are even part of our language. Consult the dictionary for the kind of descriptive adjectives assigned to women versus the adjectives assigned to men.

The result has been the normalization of this unequal treatment of men versus women. Society's acceptance of this difference is clear to the most casual of observers. Those who comply and obey are good; those who beg to differ and disobey are bad.

Each of us has the responsibility of fulfilling our maximum potential as human beings. That is what we should be communicating to generation after generation if we want a world that is healthy and peaceful. Such a message may be inconvenient for those who prefer control through manipulation, coercion and abuse but it would serve to neutralize their influence. It is fortunate for the human race that men and women are different and both have the potential to excel. We must maximize this good fortune.

LET'S STOP PRETENDING

We need to stop pretending that humans are different from animals in the wild. Our "superior brainpower" has not given us dominion over the world. We have of course created some amazing things, but any such achievements are counterbalanced by an even greater measure of destruction – of both the world and our fellow humans.

Two models stand out in my mind as explanations of why predatory and destructive forces prevail over and over again. A bell curve known as the Normal Distribution Curve shows us that less than 15% of people consider the long-term consequences of their actions. When such short-term thinking predominates, the damage we wreak as a species can be no surprise.

The second model is to be found in the work of the economist Professor Carlo M. Cipolla. His Basic Laws of Human Stupidity classifies people into 4 quadrants on a matrix:

Quadrant 1 – Helpless. They benefit others but
                  lose themselves.
Quadrant 2 – Stupids. Everyone loses.
Quadrant 3 – Bandits. Unfair benefits for themselves.
Quadrant 4 – Intelligents. Fair benefits to everyone.

Those in Group 4 are able to map the chain of causes and effects to discern the long term consequences of their actions. If you do not hone your ability to do so, you will find yourself in one of the three other quadrants.

For those who do find themselves in these other three quadrants, the future remains uncertain. If they consider it at all, they find they are unable to comprehend the forms it might take. Into such a void steps the figure of the "strong" leader, offering comfort and reassurance and the understanding the masses lack. Such "strong" leaders tap into the public hunger for certainty and simplicity in a confusing and unpredictable world. They claim that they know the answers and all we need to do is to follow their lead. With their power and puffery, too many believe their claims.

This is the Achilles heel of humanity but also its potential for long-term survival: if we can only select the right leaders, those that do possess the answers the majority of us crave, then we can prosper. The first step will be to recognize the gravity of selecting a leader. Doing so is a decision and not a simple choice, as many of the things that the leader chooses will be irreversible.

WAKE UP! LOOK FAR AND LISTEN DEEP

Human survival depends on a re-examination of our beliefs about right and wrong. We must revisit what we transmit to generation after generation through religion, education, family-values and work-'ethics'. If there is a difference between humans and animals in the wild, we need to find it, build on it and live by it. Otherwise we will end up as radioactive dust on a planet going through a long nuclear winter.

It is not foolish to be compassionate and kind. Compassion means that we are capable of thinking long term and understanding the chain of causality. We must take the time to look at how one thing leads to the next. Who will be impacted? What will be the consequences for those affected by our decisions? Do we care?

We cannot afford to dismiss the importance of rigor in decision making. Irresponsible decisions lead us down the path of mutual losses. Critical thinking that considers the implications and consequences of our decisions lead to mutual gains. Win-win is not a cliche – it is a real possibility! But where do we start and how do we accomplish it? We could begin by asking what's unique about being human? What distinguishes us from animals, machines and AI? Could it be our ability to imagine and understand the long-term benefits versus immediate gratification?

Let's start by looking at the menu of "acceptable" gender roles and dissecting how aligned or misaligned they are with the interests, capabilities and potential of individuals. Let's ask ourselves how we are contributing to the continuity and sustainability of the human race.

A LIFE FIT FOR PETS

Why are suicide rates up in developed countries? Why is life-expectancy beginning to fall back the prior heights reached due to modern medicine? Where does the exponential need to numb our feelings with alcohol and drugs come from? Just look at the urban landscape – people living in small boxes called homes, raising pets instead of families, working incessantly, and over-drinking and overeating as recreation. Have we confused human development with chicken farming?

The drop in birthrates and rise in suicide rates and early deaths are consequences of this life of "quiet desperation". It seems the feudal system never went away; it is now a sophisticated 5-Star Tax Farm and Consumption Machine designed to ensure that you stay on the treadmill and keep paying until your heart stops beating.

I wonder whether we would be better off if our societies were those of the extended family, the small tribe or small village. Did such lives offer benefits we now miss? Should we reassess how we design our lives?

There is no doubt that there was cruelty and discrimination in those contexts, but maybe in building our global world, we threw out the baby with the bathwater. But as long as we have the ability to consider and pursue different choices, there is the hope for us to live the lives that we deserve. It is our responsibility to make sure that those options are available to us.

HAVE WE LOST SIGHT OF LIFE'S PRIORITIES

Without the help of my mother when my children were still very young, I would have been in a terrible situation. There were many days when I had to take one of my sons to work with me and have him in a "play pen" in my office. How lucky to have an office and a supportive (though somewhat shocked staff) to watch over him while I was teaching. Rethinking and redesigning human-friendly environments in the world allows us to pursue our development and reach our potential.

SURRENDER OR ELSE...

A silent or silenced world that no longer knows what to believe has surrendered its power of choice. The surrender was made in the belief that it had no such power. That silent surrender assured the powerful that they had nothing to fear, and the application of social engineering in all its facets has ensured their safety.

Now their titles have changed to disguise their actual roles and protect them from harm. Those who dare to ask uncomfortable questions or challenge the status quo receive the punishments and "rewards" deemed appropriate for those stepping out of line.

Have you noticed how conveniently the sins, real, fabricated or imagined, of those stepping out of line surface? Have you also observed how they are suicided, jumping out of conveniently open windows, or have unfortunate accidents in plain sight. The media then goes into a frenzy of reporting like piranhas decimating a corpse. And the addiction to the heroin of power goes on unabated. But, how do the serfs achieve their fulfillment in this new feudalism?

NOT ALL LEADERS ARE LEADERS

Personal fulfillment and its importance in ensuring good mental health and wellbeing for both men and women is elusive in such a hostile and destructive environment. It is even more destructive when we know we have the intellectual and emotional resources to achieve our dreams and goals but never make a decision to step up and do whatever it takes to make our dreams our realities.

Many give up because belonging is more important than achieving and rejection is a terrifying prospect. History is full of examples of not giving credit where credit is due in the sciences, arts, technology, business and politics. It is enough to take a look at the capital cities of the world and compare the number of monuments celebrating the achievements of men versus those celebrating women for any reason at all.

EVEN CITIES HAVE BUILT-IN BIAS

Monuments overwhelmingly celebrate the achievements of men. When they are depicted at all, monuments of women often do not commemorate them as autonomous historical agents.

Breaking the cultural, social and personal boundaries of prescribed role definitions can be dangerous when no "legitimized" replacements are available. However, it is possible to do so. Indeed, it has been done – albeit at a high cost – by many brave women who to this day have not been given full public recognition and visibility.

CAN WE BE INDEPENDENT AND LEAD?

From as far back as I can remember, I have been seen as a natural leader. Throughout my life, I have been selected for roles of responsibility. But leadership is a double-edged sword.

Accepting a role conferred by others takes away your independence and in many ways limits your scope of action. My experience has shown me that when there is no formal role, the impact one has is far more powerful. Leadership is neither a title nor a position; it is a state of being. A model for truly effective leadership is to become a role model that others willingly and without invitation want to follow.

When there is nothing to be gained, no constituents whom you need to please or masters to bow down to, you find your true power. No one can stop you from being who you truly are. I have come to believe that each of us as humans has a vibrational signature that can be "read" on the subconscious level by other humans. We respond to one another according to the signals received on that unconscious and unspoken level.

This is the irony of leadership: when we are independent, when we stand outside of the bankrupt and corrupted models of power and domination, then and only then can we truly lead.

HISTORY REPEATS BECAUSE IT'S OUR ANCESTRAL SCRIPT

History is replete with examples of killing the independent (whether physically or morally) to protect the status quo.

Isolation and exclusion is one tool. Delaying acknowledgement of achievements until after they are dead is another, diminishing the scope of their impact.

There is no avoiding this. But you can defy it. Make your decisions and choices based on exactly what you want to achieve, with full awareness of the price you will have to pay. There is always a price to be paid to gain your independence and embrace your true identity. But the price of relinquishing your identity is even higher.

The greatest mistake we can make in life is to dim our lights and blur our identity so others don't feel diminished. No! We are who we are. We should not go out of our way to cause harm of any kind to others. However, we must fiercely defend our boundaries and work on achieving our full potential. Tough luck to those who want to write prescriptions for us so that they feel good.

Take a good look in your medicine cabinet. Whose prescriptions are you following and are they helping you? You may be slowly poisoning your chances for a happy life.

CHAPTER 7

HOW TO BE VISIBLE, SAFE AND RECOGNIZED

Diminishing ourselves so others don't see, feel inconvenienced or threatened by us is never the solution. You will earn only a lack of appreciation or recognition, and you will feel only resentment.

TIP-TOEING VISUALLY

You may be familiar with this advice; many people, most of them female, have been on the receiving end of it: *look pretty and keep your mouth shut.* That's what a lady does.

Another thing we are encouraged to do is to tip toe around people, to avoid triggering them. To make sure you are not seen or heard. To keep out of the line of fire.

This may have worked for the little girl who wants to avoid punishment, who has little scope to escape or transcend the adults who dominate her. But it doesn't serve the adult woman.

IT'S TIME TO STOP TIP-TOEING

It is important for us to be seen and heard in ways that enable us to get what we deserve in life. Diminishing ourselves invites others to treat us as if we are lesser than we truly are. When others act as if we are not there it deepens our feelings of low self-esteem. The line of causality between our behavior and attitude towards ourself is not apparent in the attitude of others. We mistakenly blame others for treating us as if we were an object and not a human.

OUR DEFENSE MECHANISMS ARE LEARNED IN CHILDHOOD

Our defense mechanisms are learned in childhood. They are driven by fear and the need to protect ourselves from real or perceived dangers, and they are also driven by our need for love and belonging and the desire to get our fair share. Each of us develops a set of behaviors that keeps us safe in different environments and in different relationships – home, school, work and social settings.

These behaviors become part of what we think is our personality, and we mistakenly assume that they cannot be changed. In reality, they are habits that can be unlearned and replaced with more supportive behaviors – behaviors that lead to a happier and calmer life with better chances for unconditional love and personal fulfillment.

ANIMALS DO IT TOO

The survival mechanism of invisibility is one of many defense responses seen in nature. The turtle is just one example. Yet these same creatures become very visible when it is time to mate and reproduce – to ensure the survival of the species and the perpetuation of that gene pool.

What happens when those humans who retreat into their shells want to be seen, appreciated, loved and recognized?

Children who resort to invisibility lose out on their share of love and belonging. Invisibility might help them avoid punishment from parents or siblings, but it also deprives them of positive attention. Every action has a price tag attached to it.

DEFENSIVE HABITS CAN IMPACT HAPPINESS

It is well worth the trouble for parents to familiarize themselves with the full range of children's defensive behaviors. They should consider how to relate to their children in more supportive ways. It is critical to do so before destructive habits get hardwired. These unconscious habits can destroy the future happiness of their children.

The greatest fallacy we live with is the assumption that parenting is a purely biological process and parenting is instinctive. It is not! There is no excuse for ignorance in a world drowning in information and insights about human development, psychology and emotional wellbeing. And if we decide not to use this knowledge, it does not mean that it is not used against us. It is masterfully applied in advertising, propaganda, warfare and psyops, for the control or destruction of others.

WE NEED AN ANTI-MANIPULATION VACCINE

Parents need to be educated in the fullest and deepest sense of the word.

It is their responsibility to equip themselves with the techniques of effective parenting, and supported with communication skills and emotional intelligence. We have advanced beyond anyone's widest dreams in technology and regressed beyond anyone's widest dreams as higher-order beings.

There is so much for us to unlearn from our childhood. We need to reassess what we do and how we do it, and we must continue to examine this on a regular basis. We must distinguish between those habits that serve us and those that hurt us. Once aware of these, we must replace those habits with ones that give us inner strength and self-confidence. The parenting journey never ends. Just as our journey of self-discovery, growth and development should never end.

THE CURSE OF SISYPHUS

For better or for worse, parents stay with us forever. Parents are part of our DNA, our psyche, our habits, our words – our entire model of reality. If we do not understand this, and break free from those patterns of behavior that hurt us and hurt others, we are doomed to the same fate as Sisyphus in Greek mythology, doomed not only to forever repeat the same futile patterns of behavior, but to pass them on to the next generation whether they help or hurt us.

It is extremely hard to break away from unconscious patterns of behavior without gnawing feelings of guilt. It is even harder to break free from the more subtle scotoma of things that appear perfect only because we don't see the flaws.

It is our right and our responsibility to ensure that our children are better versions of ourselves and their children better versions of them. This is how we can realize humanity's full potential; this is what it means to be human and to build together a world that is less fearful, greedy and destructive. If AI can perform so many of the operational tasks of day to day life, what is our role as human beings if not this?

IS THERE AN ANTIDOTE TO DESTRUCTION?

Are there any antidotes to destructive habits? Not only is the answer an emphatic yes, but it is of fundamental importance we pursue them. It is our sacred duty to make continuous learning and growth foundational to our lives and the lives we touch. It is our highest responsibility as intelligent humans to treat other humans with respect and compassion and do what we can to elevate them and build their – and our own – self-esteem in the process.

None of our possessions will follow us to the grave. All that remains are the memories and behaviors of those whose lives we have touched, positively or negatively. Our wealth does not define us, nor does it ever fill the bottomless void of those who hunger for it. The wealth of the Pharaohs was buried with them, only for it to be plundered so others could cash in.

PEACE IS POSSIBLE IF GREED IS CURBED

If only we could learn from history, we could build a world that is peaceful and cooperative. We simply need to connect the dots that lead from aggression and destruction to their logical conclusion. Tracing the line of causality that has played and replayed for millennia will always lead you to the same end: MAD – mutually assured destruction. Every generation should trace and re-trace this chain, so what is at stake is never forgotten.

Yet our education in history is often more fictional than factual. Why at this particular time and for what particular purpose and for which particular generation was history framed and re-made?

EMPOWERED OR POWERLESS IS A CHOICE

We must first understand the missteps of our own histories. We must learn and apply the lessons they teach us.

Instead of keeping a low profile and disengaging emotionally, we should become strategic and network with mutual respect, expressing ourselves with authenticity and sincerity, and leading others towards their own self-belief.

Instead of being challenging and aggressive, we must show compassion and kindness towards others, allowing ourselves and others to communicate and share with a sense of openness and trust.

Instead of desperately performing for the approval of others, we should creatively express our inner thoughts and feelings, exploring ideas and concepts that empower others.

Parents can facilitate such transformations by becoming best friends with their now adult children. They must admit their past mistakes, engage in conversations, make sense of the past in light of the present and try out practical scenarios for future action. The need for unconditional love and acceptance never goes away, nor does the need for impartial conflict resolution among siblings.

ONCE A PARENT, NOW A BEST FRIEND

So if you are fortunate enough to be alive when your children are adults, use your unconditional love to become the healer who soothes past hurts and missteps, the permission-giver who helps remove the shackles of the past.

The joke that says "parents allow their children to be themselves as long as they do it their way" has a lot of truth to it. So make your way a better way and guide your adult children towards it. Have those difficult conversations with your adult children while you have the luxury of doing so.

Like everything in life, we need to measure progress in order to confirm that it is genuine. We need to check that we are not living in a Fool's Paradise where we believe that all is well when it is not. In my life, and in the lives of my children, many of our behaviors have changed over time, which in turn has given me great hope that things will become even better as time passes, as experience deepens and everyone continues to learn and grow.

My children have learned to acknowledge one another's achievements and capabilities, leading to open and respectful conversations in which requests for help are heeded and respected.

They have learned to offer forgiveness for past mistakes, and how to move on towards understanding, compassion, love and practical companionship.

They have discovered that there is no need to compete with anyone except themselves, to step into their own power and believe that they are loved for who they are – no proof needed.

And I have learned to recognize that each child has become a competent, capable and more visible adult. I have learned to see myself in the personal brilliance that others see, reward and promote.

OBSOLESCENCE APPLIES TO BELIEFS TOO

It is vital that we dislodge obsolete beliefs and replace them with empowering ones. Otherwise we will only repeat and replay the destructive patterns of the past. Becoming aware of a destructive pattern is the first step to shattering and replacing it with a better and healthier alternative.

Resting is a mental process, not a physical one. Breaking old patterns is foundational to achieving mental rest and freedom from stress. Just as we need to water plants, prune them and provide nutrients so that they maintain their vibrancy, we need to cultivate ourselves. We must do it for the sake of our wellbeing.

We need to acknowledge our own achievements, to remind ourselves of those qualities we wish to build on, and to select the ones we want to leave in the past so that we can work towards more fulfilling ones in the future. Learning and growth never stops; they must be a daily practice until our very last breath.

UNDERSTANDING IS A CATALYST FOR UNCONDITIONAL LOVE

I have great confidence that actions emerging from maturity and experience will assure better futures and relationships for my family.

Greater compassion for self and family, stopping and enjoying periods of relaxation without guilt, kindness instead of judgment, the recognition that things do not have to be perfect, the belief that we are good enough and have nothing to prove to anyone... These behaviors indicate deeper understanding of self and others.

This kind of understanding is a catalyst for unconditional love and acceptance of ourselves and others. Our ability to learn and grow is our greatest resource for resilience. Remembering that we can make better choices next time is the key that unlocks the gate of our mental prison.

CHAPTER 8

UNLOCK THE GATE AND SET YOURSELF FREE

You live in a cell of your beliefs. That cell has a gate. That gate has a lock. But only you can find the key, place the key in the lock, turn it and set yourself free.

FIND THE KEY AND UNLOCK THE GATE

Unlock the gate and walk free; just walk away when you choose. Mental prisons can be even more secure than the best maximum-security prisons, but only because most of us are not even aware we are locked within them. The prison is inside of us; it has remained within us so long that we think it is simply part of our lives.

Far too many of us live and die without ever realizing that we spent our lives in unnecessary solitary confinement. We believed there was some higher power in control, or that we were simply born at the wrong time, in the wrong place, to the wrong parents, simply the victims of bad luck!

UNDERSTANDING THE PATTERNS

As I look back at my own life, I can say that I know very little of the history of my parents. They were far ahead of their time, liberal thinkers for their generation, and loving parents. However, they were reading from a script of what was considered best practice for parenting at the time.

As a child, I did not comprehend how important it was to understand how my parents' life journeys brought them to where they were. As a result, I didn't capture and document stories of their life experiences. They shared some of their stories with me and my siblings as a form of entertainment, but I missed the significance at the time. Reconstruction from memory is a poor substitute as I look back in my later years.

OUR PROGRAMMING CAN BE INSIDIOUS

When we do not understand and appraise, what remains is the old programming, the unconscious copying of old repetitions. We shouldn't be surprised when family histories repeat generation after generation. I was taken aback when listening to an interview of a second cousin whom I had only met for just a few minutes, during one of my trips to Jamaica. She was espousing the exact same values that we hold dear as a family! How did those same values get so firmly embedded in her thoughts, speech and behavior?

Sadly I no longer have the opportunity to preserve the wisdom of my ancestors, to appraise the lessons of obsolete rules of engagement. But I might have done, once upon a time. The opportunities passed by silently like shadows in the night, falling on the deaf ears of my teenage self.

Old rules, helpful and unhelpful, linger somewhere in the recesses of our subconscious. This is why it is important for me to share my own experiences in this book so my children, grandchildren and even great grand-children can answer, if they choose, that perennial question, "How did we get here?"

I hope it will help them to do a better job of sorting the helpful programming from the unhelpful. My hope is that they will use this book to do what is most important: to reset their expectations of themselves and for themselves. This is an opportunity that is open to all of us. If you are reading this book, it is important to you too.

RESETTING AND RESTING IS A MENTAL PROCESS

Resetting is like releasing the tension on the bowstring, allowing it to return to its natural resting position. The tension is the mental strain that comes from adhering to arbitrary rules. We adhere to many such rules due only to our fear of rejection. We do not take time to adequately assess the value of those rules to the quality of our lives. Freedom from fear is a mental and not a physical process.

We are programmed – educated, socialized and conditioned – to believe things that make it convenient for us to be managed and controlled. The controllers are whoever is in charge of the power structures that surround us. The rules and control mechanisms are determined by the culture we reside in. When we move from culture to culture, we have to adjust to the new structures and rules.

Yet we are always looking for the paradisiacal environment which will solve all our problems. We must realize that no such paradise exists. We must build it ourselves. Developing our humanity, improving human relations and evolving towards understanding and cooperation are the path to this paradise. This approach to life is within the power of each individual, family, community and country. All that is needed is for us to use our human ingenuity for construction instead of destruction. Why don't we choose humanization over baboonization? I wonder.

OBEDIENCE AND COMPLIANCE ARE DANGEROUS

Unquestioning obedience and compliance can be as dangerous, if not more dangerous than disobedience and non-compliance. Obedience and compliance keep us locked in a world created for the convenience and survival of others.

Such a world is by necessity black and white. There can be no flexibility because that would introduce ambiguity, opening the possibility of stepping out of line without punishment. Now that would certainly pose a threat to the controllers. The safety and longevity of those controllers depend on the belief that there are no safe or viable alternatives to the status quo. Luckily for them, many obligingly accept this as truth and pass on this belief to the next generation.

I discovered this system of obedience and compliance during religious studies classes as a child. It felt like I was being asked to accept so many contradictory pieces of information, stories that felt no different from the mythology of any other civilization. I sought to understand how we got here and why things are the way they are, yet the answers I received made no sense at all. It was as if I was being asked to believe in magic.

Why can't we look at the principles and values that keep us human? Why can't we learn how to build better relationships and preserve social order through mutual compassion, rather than fear of punishment? Is fear of others, the need for retribution and spiritual psychopathy the best past to preserve and expand our humanity?

PLEASE STAY AWAY

In college, I was eventually asked to stop attending religious studies classes, even though attendance was supposed to be mandatory. Instead I was instructed only to sit the final exam. I asked too many uncomfortable and potentially disruptive questions. In the eyes of the professor, it was certainly better to remove me from the cohort of obedient and compliant students.

But not all of the class that remained were simply obedient. Only later did I learn the secrets of the chameleon called compliance. I discovered that some colleagues were very good at becoming chameleons for survival, rather than simple obedience.

THINKING IS POTENTIALLY LIFE THREATENING

That survival mechanism is simple: "Tell them what they want to hear." Sometimes the cost of not doing so is either too high or a waste of time. Thinking is a dangerous and potentially life-threatening activity.

The only other course in which I performed badly during my years at college was political science. I still hadn't learned how to be "smart". I earned an F for my answer to the question "What is the difference between Democracy and Communism?" My answer was that the difference was in the methodology applied to achieve the same outcome: obedience and compliance.

The democratic approach is to give the individual everything up front and have them work their tails off for thirty or forty years to settle the debt. The communistic approach is to have them work their tails off to procure material rewards and other benefits. In both systems, individuals must stay focused on the goal of avoiding a miserable life. The outcome, as I said, was two different forms of feudalism, only with different labels. It made me laugh when I first heard the term "Techno Feudalism" and later read the book by Yanis Varoufakis with the same title.

WHAT IS POOR JUDGEMENT? WHAT IS GOOD?

On the subject of religion, I later researched the correlation between the seasons and their climatic changes with the timing of the various religious beliefs and celebrations. And I wrote a full masters thesis entitled "A Study of the Archetypal Patterns of the Persephone Myth in Selected Works by Henry James". For this thesis, I received outstanding marks and was invited to expand and co-publish it with my professor in a leading literary journal, before continuing for a PhD at Oxford University in the UK. I declined both suggestions because it was not what I wanted to do with my life. Was that good judgement or poor judgement?

Knowing what you don't want doesn't mean that you know what you do want. Examine your beliefs. Where did they come from and who did you receive and accept them from? You are no longer a child and must reassess what you were told when you didn't know any better. Beliefs only have power if we accept them as truths. The locked gate is our beliefs. That gate remains firmly shut unless we work on unlocking it.

MASTERING YOUR FEAR IS THE KEY

If we never examine our beliefs and determine what to keep and what to discard, we remain locked behind that gate. Our fear of loss and our need for certainty play a huge role in keeping us in solitary confinement. These two forces are not to be underestimated.

However, if you dare to overcome your fears, you will be able to unlock the gate and venture outside. And you may discover that not only can you survive but thrive as you become bolder and bolder and move further and further beyond the gate. You might move so far that it vanishes into the distance, becoming no more than a memory.

SKEPTICISM IS VALUABLE

A wise old man once shared with me a timeless piece of wisdom: "Believe half of what you see and none of what you hear."

After the birth of my second son, my lower back was causing me so much pain that I couldn't walk. I was lifted into the car and taken to the emergency room at the hospital. The attending physician, a surgeon, told me that if I did not have urgent surgery on my back, I would be paralyzed. Given the context – wartime, a hospital in a small town, my utter exhaustion working two jobs and sleeping for an average of four hours a night for many months – I begged to differ.

I said that I would take my chances with an alternative course of action, and if it didn't work, we would revisit the possibility of surgery. I spent two weeks on my back on a hard floor. I was given injections to manage the pain and keep the nerves in my lower back properly supplied with the analgesics and vitamins necessary. As soon as I could move again, I took up swimming and lying down on the warm summer sand of the beach as often as possible.

I have never had that surgery on my back. I had two other children and continue to be physically fit to this day.

RESPONSIBILITY IS ONE OF THE STRONGEST MEDICATIONS

The responsibility of supporting and raising four children is no small task. That responsibility took me to places where few would consider going. The pressure of a civil war which paralyzed my country and destabilized the region contributed to my choices. Few people, let alone a woman flying solo, would be prepared to visit many of those places. But I am sure that those of you who take a responsibility pill three times a day have also done many things that surprise you when you look back at your lives.

I lived in Lebanon then and continue to live in Lebanon now because it is my country. I have been to every corner of my country and worked with friends and foes alike. I delivered groundbreaking projects, touched thousands of lives for the better, and I am proud of the impact my work has had. I am even prouder of relationships I forged. Such is the power of responsibility.

LUCK IS THE PATH TO DISAPPOINTMENT

I have completed projects in Syria, Yemen, Kuwait, Bahrain, Jordan, Oman, the Emirates, Africa, Europe, the USA, Malaysia, Thailand, Japan; I have been to the Kingdom of Saudi Arabia when it was mandatory for women to cover themselves from head to toe; I worked in Iraq during the invasion of that country, driving across the desert in four-wheel SUVs, evacuated on ten minutes' notice from the green zone, returning to Jordan over land in a grueling twenty-four hour drive.

Yet I have always felt protected. I have always returned to my family in one piece. Our relationship with our children contributes greatly to the size of their comfort zone and appetite for risk. Many of you probably ask yourselves whether or not your approach to parenting helped or hindered the course of your children's lives. I don't know the answer to those questions. What I do know is that as long as we can unlearn and relearn, there is hope.

Some people describe survival of adversity as luck. I honestly do not know what luck is. Perhaps it is simply a concept to prevent us from going crazy because the thought that we really do not have any control is so terrifying. Ultimately chance and probability govern whether you find yourself in the wrong place at the wrong time or in the right place at the right time.

THESE MUSHROOM CLOUDS WERE NOT SPECIAL EFFECT

I was not in the theatre but I had a front seat view. It was a chance to see how little control we really have. We have no control over these things. You could be sitting peacefully in your living room, as I was, when I heard rumbling deep inside the earth. My panoramic window, looking out at what a moment ago was a peaceful blue Mediterranean Sea, began to vibrate. I got off my couch just in time to escape the shattering glass and blown out window. I saw the red, black and grey mushroom clouds of the Beirut Port explosion in slow motion.

Lives, businesses, history and the potential for peace were blown to smithereens in an instant. We do not control what happens outside or even inside of ourselves from moment to moment. It is impossible to comprehend, to hold in your mind for any period of time this lack of predictability and control for any period of time without falling apart.

TUNNEL VISION IS A RESPONSE TO FEAR

As I drove through a potentially mined banana plantation at night, I had tunnel vision, focusing on the one meter ahead of me. I was intent on getting out of the banana plantation and onto the road that would take me safely back home to my children. If I thought for one minute about being blown up by a landmine or shot by a sniper, I couldn't have done it.

And yet I felt protected. I felt that some unknown and undefined positive force was keeping me safe. I felt the same way when I handed a case file to the VP for academic affairs, whom I accused of unethical practices and misappropriation of funds. This feeling that I am living in an alternative reality, in a movie, comes back every time I do difficult things.

Life outside the gate is the journey of realizing your full potential. To keep honing your skill, will and determination, to pursue and realize your goals, is the best path to independence and self-reliance. Perhaps it is our commitment to this path that assures us, even in moments of danger, that we are protected – that we are doing the right thing.

UNLOCK THE GATE

I have always wanted to write books, but I told myself that survival was a greater priority, or that what I had to say was not important, or that it had all been said before. Those were some of the obstacles I put in my own path. Now at seventy-eight, I am doing it.

Your beliefs are the gate to that maximum security prison and fear is the lock on that solitary confinement cell. Getting over your fear and using that courage is the key to unlocking both the cell and the gate. It is the key to setting yourself free.

CHAPTER 9

STRATEGIC AND DETAIL-ORIENTED OUTLIERS

What happens when you see both the big picture and the details? Does it make communication better or worse? How does this duality shape your relationships and your ability to communicate in a language accessible to others?

WHAT ON EARTH ARE YOU TALKING ABOUT?

If you are among the minority who see both the big picture and the fine details, you face some unique challenges. Some of these challenges are internal, others external. When you speak with yourself, you may ask, "What's *the* point?" But when you speak with others, they may ask, "What's *your* point?"

It can be difficult to maintain your motivation when you find only a small circle relates to your thinking. It can make you more cautious than necessary, mistakenly concluding that what you are doing doesn't make sense.

Even if you are not discouraged, being ahead of the curve can mean that you do not benefit from your own initiatives. It depends on others' perceptions of risk and opportunity.

DIFFERENCES ARE ESSENTIAL FOR SURVIVAL

Our thoughts and beliefs generate feelings and those feelings lead to actions. The actions we take produce our history. We weave a story that we tell ourselves about this history, about the reasons for our successes and failures as we see them.

If we accept our stories as realities, instead of fictional explanations, then we find ourselves in a mental prison of our own making. The Greek philosopher Heraclitus (535-475 BC) is credited with the quote "character is destiny". We should beware then, lest the characters we build for ourselves consign us to miserable futures.

DO YOU KNOW WHO YOU ARE?

We can have better lives if we understand ourselves and if we master three things.

First we must develop the skill of reining in our reactions, our reflexive emotions.

Second, we must consider the consequences of our actions.

Third, we must make more responsible choices before responding thoughtfully to situations.

It is no small achievement to master these three things.

Learning to respond instead of react is a lifelong process and a foundational requirement for better relations with ourselves and others.

SURVIVAL IS STATISTICAL

Through the process of evolution, nature has ensured a distribution of qualities among human populations. This distribution ensures slow but continual progress. This progress is the result of the pushes forward provided by the minority of adventurous thinkers who want to go ahead of the curve. It is counterbalanced by the pull back of the ultraconservatives who want to stick to the tried and tested. Then there is the large majority, who maintain certainty and stability through small, measured safe changes.

The smallest percentage are those who want to move faster and further, imagining the future, creating, innovating and experimenting. They see the big picture and the potential for improvement. They also dive enthusiastically into the details of how to transform their ideas into realities.

These are the potential disruptors. However, they represent such a small percentage that it takes one or more generations for their ideas to become mainstream. Too often, when they share their ideas with the majority, they are thought of as mad.

ONE MAN'S MADNESS IS ANOTHER MAN'S GENIUS

It is not madness. It is this dual ability to see both the big picture and the fine details.

The ability to relate and integrate many different areas of knowledge and emerge with a vision of the future is not common. These abilities look very mysterious to those who do not see how the dots are connected. They don't see the premises from which you analyzed, so they don't see how the conclusions you formed are explicable. The outcome is predictable: "How did you arrive at this conclusion?"

But it would be a mistake to conclude that those asking such questions are stupid. No, it is just a different way of processing the world. Both ways of thinking are valuable and complementary.

CONNECTING TOO MANY DOTS LOOKS SUSPICIOUS

No, I am not a witch or a secret service agent. I connected the dots, I discarded the unsubstantiated information, and I took things to their logical conclusion.

How do I know all this about you? I know because you just told me. I was listening with intent and depth. I listened with genuine interest – interest in both you and in the subject of which you spoke.

My PA used to tell me that faculty members found me scary, asking if she could please serve as the go-between. It is feedback that has been repeated to me over and over.

I was told it was as if I had x ray vision. So rarely do we listen to each other that, when we do, it is mistaken for some kind of magic.

YOU CAN ONLY BE YOU

So often did I receive the same complaints, at one time I thought it would be a good thing if I lowered my profile. I thought that others would feel more comfortable. This strategy succeeded in situations where others wanted a neutral go-between. It failed in situations that needed an accurate understanding of context and requirements. It also caused me to lose business.

Never try to be someone you are not. It robs you of your authenticity, and it is obvious to those observing you. It is not worth the effort or the stress to play a role that was not meant for you. How many times have you discovered that being true to yourself is the only effective way forward?

The greatest mistake I have made in life is to diminish myself so that others would not feel intimidated. If I had stopped following the formula of trying to diminish myself much earlier in life, I would have been far wealthier in financial terms.

IT REALLY IS MIND OVER MONEY

Not that the financials would have mattered. The money in Lebanon's banks has disappeared, leaving only a digital record of what once was there. I and hundreds of thousands of other depositors do not know if we will ever see our money again.

I am grateful that I never depended on money. No, I depended on my ability to make money. Money comes from your capabilities and your brainpower. It comes from problem-solving, not falling into despair.

Balancing the long view with an understanding of details requires you to live with one foot in the present, one in the future. Your understanding of the future must be your compass; your understanding of the present provides you with the raw material for action.

The juggler of the present and the future can do what many others find quite daunting.

Thinking that the amount of money we have is the only indicator of success is dangerous. What happens if that money is lost through devaluation, embezzlement, sanctions or criminal governments? Do you suddenly become unworthy or incompetent? No. The most valuable currency you own is your competence, resourcefulness and resilience.

What are your indicators of success? Do your indicators build your value or devalue you in your own eyes?

CULTIVATE YOUR MIND WITH PUZZLE BUILDING

I have learned so much from the businesses and projects I have been involved in. The signs were there from my earliest years. Do you remember the things that mattered to you as a child? Too often we forget the qualities that formed us.

As a little girl, I found business and commerce exciting. I enjoyed going to my parents' retail store and participating in all the different aspects of the business: sales, money management, stock-taking and similar activities.

When my parents sold their business in Jamaica and returned to Lebanon, it never occurred to them that anyone other than their son was capable of taking over the business. When my brother made it clear that it was not his ambition to be in the retail business, my parents sold it. Yet that childhood experience was not wasted. Look closely, and you will see that every part of your life is a piece of the puzzle that you will finally assemble into who you become.

As a young wife and mother in my mid-twenties, I worked closely with my husband to set up a factory for the production of extractor fans. My husband was an electro-mechanical engineer and thought that if we set up manufacturing in Lebanon and distributed our products throughout the Middle East, we would be rich and successful.

We set up the factory, manufactured from basic materials and produced fractional horsepower motors. We used these motors as the main part in the extractor fans the factory produced. This kind of manufacturing was something never before done in Lebanon. A technological achievement and a first in the country according to the ministry of industry.

Then the civil war broke out. Life was a non-stop nightmare. These were years of accidents, injuries, debts, savage competition, bombs and shrapnel, followed by financial ruin. Yet while the learning curve was steep and painful, it was nevertheless valuable.

If character is destiny, is it because I love my independence so much that I have had all these experiences? Or is it because I have had all these experiences that I have become fiercely independent?

What is the role that encompasses all that you have done or not done? Is this the title of your character?

PIONEER SEEMS TO FIT

My one-size-fits-all title is pioneer. The projects in which I was a pioneer are many. After the collapse of the extractor fan venture, they all revolved around education.

I established the English language section of a well-known French language school, designing, testing and implementing the curriculum from KG to high school. I also taught the classes to ensure that the program was meeting the pedagogical requirements.

I then established an English language adult education program for the parents and young adults of the Francophone community. This was necessary so that they could learn and support their children in the English language section of the school. Later, those of university age would be eligible to enter the American-style university that was a future project. This "Open Half a Hemisphere" project was a huge success because of its creative teaching techniques applied to adult education.

Next I established a university based on the American system. I connected the president of the American university with the head of the monastic order who owned the school, securing funding for the establishment of the first English-language university in the region. I served as business planner, project manager, registrar, advisor, instructor, and I don't remember how many other roles.

FROM START TO FINISH, OVER AND OVER...

I was fully involved with the first seventy-five students who enrolled. Several of these students are still in touch with me. I stayed for seventeen years and worked tirelessly for ten to twelve hours a day until this institution became a full-scale university accredited by the State of New York. Today course credits can be transferred between this university and most universities in the USA.

I served in many different academic positions, the last of which was dean of the faculty of humanities. But then, after three years of agonizing internal debate with myself, I tendered my resignation and walked away, forgoing free university education for my children and a lifetime job guarantee.

I then set up a business of my own, the Academy of English, the purpose of which was to teach English that would enable graduates to achieve the level of fluency necessary to study abroad and qualify for different professional certifications – engineering, law, medicine, etc. I kept this business going for twenty-five years, opening up branches, and offering nationwide education consultancy services. And once English language teaching became mainstream, commoditized and no longer a challenge for me, I decided to do something more fulfilling.

Next I established a management consultancy business in which I am still deeply involved today. This business has evolved over a period of thirty-two years, going through multiple local, regional and international metamorphoses. Today we are a UK-registered partnership and focus on leadership, strategic communication and business emotional intelligence.

PIONEERING IS NOT NECESSARILY AN ADVANTAGE

Always being the pioneer puts you at a disadvantage: there is no roadmap for what has yet to be travelled. You must become your own lab rat. Others who come after you can learn from your successes and failures, copying what you have done twenty years later, when the public is ready.

Experiential learning with role reversal in teacher training, way back in the 80s; HR consultancy and change management in regions that hadn't heard of HR management, let alone human capital… Back then, I was always the only one from the Middle East in international conferences and events. There are so many other examples it would be tedious to remember, let alone retell.

Seeing generations repeat patterns is a blessing and a curse. When life becomes predictable and human behavior a repeat-performance, you must look hard for the ingredients of change and hope. Innovation always comes back to parenting and education. Garbage in = garbage out; good in = gold out. The question is who decides what is garbage and what is good?

COMPARTMENTALIZE AND DANCE WITH DANGER

Narrow your focus, compartmentalize and ensure that what you are doing leads to a tangible, measurable and positive result for those within your circle of influence. These people will expand the ripples as they too live by their values.

How do I know this? By raising four children during a civil war. Despite having to change schools to escape the bombs, my children were still able to develop higher order thinking. They were able to thrive in an environment where we compartmentalized, as best we could, keeping the chaos of war as minimal as possible.

The things that helped included maintaining a mini zoo at home, raising a large family of dogs, practicing arts and crafts, studying science and staging experiments, learning to cook and garden, and escaping into nature. By maintaining such projects together, we were able to maintain a positive focus on learning and growth, despite the chaos around us,

When you teach students with their guns in the classroom, you learn some of the best survival skills of all. Stories, jokes and examples that awaken critical thinking with laughter: these are amazing antidotes to potential violence. One of my favourite essays, "Love is a Fallacy" by Max Shulman, was another tonic, reminding me always to keep the warmth of family life central to my life and outlook. Kindness and compassion are antidotes to hatred and fear. They allow us to build a space of focus, learning and growth even among the chaos of war.

Opening minds with critical thinking and provocative questioning is another powerful tool, an antidote to propaganda when done in the Socratic style. Slow, persistent and kind questioning chips away at the mental calcification of false assumptions. When done with compassion, this enables both the questioner and the responder to discover themselves through personal insights. That is how false assumptions are replaced with a more balanced view of any particular situation.

CHAPTER 10

KINDNESS AND COMPASSION ARE ACTS OF BRAVERY

It takes strength to be kind, the kind of strength that comes from courage and not from force. Courage requires that we are not afraid of differences, and kindness requires an understanding of the necessity of differences for a healthy world. Homogeneity leads to genetic atrophy both figuratively and literally.

COMPASSION COMES FROM STRENGTH

Kindness and compassion are strengths. They are not signs of weakness or stupidity. The desire to hurt and humiliate others comes from a very dark place, from troubled and damaged psyches. Such psyches are driven by fear and self-loathing projected onto others. The belief that the only way to project strength is through destruction and subjugation is in and of itself the output of inner weakness. Such behavior is based on the fear that, unless we destroy things that are unfamiliar to us, our own existence is under threat.

When the protagonists and the antagonists to a conflict share the view that things that are different or unfamiliar constitute threats to be destroyed, we have big problems. It is even worse when this view of "reality" is used to scare entire communities into accepting these beliefs as truths. This is the recipe for brutal, existential conflicts.

If you have ever asked yourself whether an action was malice or stupidity, you know people do things that defy logical explanation. In such situations, the only outcome is lose-lose. The root of dysfunctional aggression is low self-esteem. It is the fear that the small, frightened, self-loathing child that still lives within the adult could be forced to face humiliation.

Do we contribute to destroying or building self-esteem – our own and that of others? Thoughtless throwaway remarks can sting like poisoned darts. We must lessen the throwing and improve the deflection. It takes courage and compassion to even consider understanding those persons and things we perceive as threats. When we resist the urge to lash out, to combat, to destroy, we exhibit that courage.

SHOULD WE BUILD OR DESTROY?

The most sacred responsibility of individuals, families, communities and countries is to understand the power of healthy self-esteem and self-confidence. I am not talking about patronizing awards for nothing. I am talking about building healthy, stable people and prosperous communities. To do this, we need to set measurable or observable standards.

No, this is not naïveté! We have used religion, education, xenophobia, and law and order to divide and conquer by cultivating hatred and fear. Such systems all have their own metrics to categorize and divide. In the same way, we can employ the antidotes to these toxic and corrosive methods of subjugation and destruction. Why can't we, every one of us, use our capabilities to build? What's stopping you?

Inner strength gives us the capability to enable others to rise, to become more competent and confident without feeling threatened or diminished. If the best we can do is to destroy and diminish, if this is the only way we can feel good about ourselves, we deserve to be replaced by AI. And if we are threatened by the success of others, we have already embarked on an inexorable journey towards mutually assured destruction. History tells us that humanity has been there and done that many times over, and still we have not learned a single thing.

WE KEEP RESETTING TO THE STONE AGE

Still we keep resetting the clock back to the Stone Age. My gun is bigger than your gun and my daddy is stronger than your daddy – how pathetic, how unfitting for an intelligent human being.

Finding the core of who we truly are, and embracing a positive purpose, no matter how modest, is the path to incredible self-confidence. From such a position, we can defend humanity. We can overcome the actions of sick, fragile egos. The lives of many men and women have been brutally destroyed by such egos, by those who feel threatened by the success of others.

BE THE HERO IN YOUR STORY

A powerful therapeutic approach is to create stories in which you are the hero. I have helped many a client with this process. Many of these people are brilliant and competent leaders who simply didn't yet realise they are exactly what they need to be. Dismissive behavior, a thousand subtle humiliations, verbal and behavioral abuse – all of these tools had been used to chip away at their self-esteem, by insecure leaders desperate to keep their underlings in check. In turn, the abused risked becoming the abuser. Personalized stories in which the victims overcome adversity and become the heroes help inoculate against this process, restoring their self-esteem.

How many of you receive regular doses of humiliation, meted out by a boss with low esteem? How do you defend your boundaries? How do you find better alternatives and boldly walk away? And how many of you stay and endure, telling yourself that this humiliation is a necessary part of survival? It is not!

Write your own story in which you are the hero. Explore how you have conquered your fears. Unlock your gate and walk free!

"More than thirty-five years ago I had my first conscious encounter with fear. Today, I am still wrestling with that fear because I am determined to change that wrestling into dancing with fear.

"I realize now that fear is my friend because it forces me to dig deep and discover resources I never knew I had. Each time I emerge from the crucible of fear and shame, I am stronger, more courageous and, ironically, more compassionate.

"The night was dark and cold, snow was all around and a stray dog was following me. My eight-year-old heart was beating so fast, I thought it would burst out of my chest. I kept on walking. I had a goal. I needed to get milk for my baby brother because there was no milk at home.

"I returned with the milk and a recognition, still vague but crystallizing: I am the pillar of my family, even at the tender age of eight. I am the pillar supporting a drunken and irresponsible father, a sick mother and a helpless infant brother.

"My purpose is to be the protector of my soul and the pillar of my family.

"I am the willow tree bending in the wind and bouncing back, alive and resilient. I am the tigress, hunting in the night and dancing with my fear, my friend."

OR BE THE BOSS OF YOUR BOSS

When a very successful person falls ill or has some temporary setback, the sharks come out to hunt. They see the temporary misfortune of the otherwise successful person as an opportunity to take control of things. They use the difficulty of the person by whom they feel threatened as legitimization for their unjustified actions.

How many of you have faced similar situations? Did you fight back or did you give in? I know some who have had to go into therapy or take prescription drugs to cope with the damage such relationships inflicted upon them. When you forget that you always have the power of choice, you lose every time. Turn around and confront those who use knowledge of your temporary vulnerability to put you down. Move them out of your path or get out of their path.

In situations like these, it is easier to write with a cool head rather than to confront someone in person. Make an assertive and clear dissection of the situation and ask for your legitimate rights. Put into writing what would have been hard to articulate otherwise.

First, state the purpose of your written communication as clearly and concisely as you can.

Second, always give the benefit of the doubt to the person you feel is treating you unfairly. Give them a way to save face. Assume positive intent and articulate specifically what you think that good intention might be.

Third, remind them of the contributions you have made and especially of the fact that your capabilities are still intact. State that you continue to deliver results and invite them to offer helpful feedback in areas where they think you are slipping.

Next, let them know how you feel at this time. Invite them to become your supporter, the confidant that you need. Remind them again of your achievements and especially of your ongoing contribution. Most importantly, remind them of the intellectual capital you share with the wider group and the value of protecting that.

Finally, ask very specifically for what you want and provide practical steps for transforming your proposed plan of action into a functioning process or application.

And remember: it requires courage and compassion to recognize oneself and stand up for one's personal and professional boundaries.

COMPASSION COMBINES UNDERSTANDING AND FEELINGS

Exercising compassion towards another requires a combination of understanding and feeling for others, whether they are stronger or weaker than we are. It also requires overcoming our fears. It takes a sufficiently healthy ego and robust self-esteem to fully embrace our identity without needing to compare ourselves to others. We can admire others and even model some of the aspects of their behaviors that will help us grow. We do not need to detract from or destroy the success of others to feel better about ourselves. We also do not need to put ourselves down because we are different. We are just that – different!

Compassion is not competition or comparison, the addition or subtraction of superiority versus inferiority. It is about understanding and growing from the position we are in to the place we want to be. How terrible to live with a malignant tumor of hidden shame, a gnawing sense of inferiority all our lives, and how liberating when the tumor is removed.

SURGICALLY REMOVE THAT TUMOR

I saw this in practice when a fifty-six-year-old president finally shared with me a hidden shame he had never shared with anyone.

This fear of exposure, to family, friends and his organization, haunted him for years. His deep breath of relief, when he realized that what he experienced was normal, in fact fairly common, was palpable. Non-judgemental and compassionate support went a long way to draining the emotional poison.

Another person I worked with shared the hidden shame of the multiple "perverted" sexual violations they had permitted in order to get ahead. Instead of further eroding his self-esteem, we found the path to recovery through relocation and a change of professional activity. Their new activities included volunteer work helping youth who might themselves face similar sexual violations and career abuse.

THE KING MAKERS OWN THE KINGS

Growth is not just physical and mental but emotional and spiritual. Feeling safe and protected in the world requires having no skeletons in the closet, either because you have removed them or because they were never there in the first place. A clean closet is a tremendous source of personal strength and emotional liberation.

Not owing your success to a "broker" to whom you sold your soul is another source of strength. As we progress through life, it is inevitable that we are lured into the false promises of many "success-brokers". While we are still in search of our true identity, not yet emerged from the muddy waters of confusion, we are easy prey. Fear of disapproval, loss of love, status, security and significance all contribute, these fears all the more potent when we haven't yet formed our own beliefs.

FEAR OF THE PAST IS MALIGNANT

Fear of our past is a source of weakness, a growing tumor of hidden shame. Finding courage, self-compassion and non-judgemental support is incredibly liberating.

When we overcome our fears, our past has no power over us. We can say what was unsayable: "I had an abusive and alcoholic husband who physically brutalized one of our children, threatening to kill the child if I intervened, leaving the rest of the family with feelings of fear, guilt and shame."

Freedom from that horror took courage, compassion and a long journey of healing and understanding.

NO ONE IS FREE UNTIL THEY ARE

Working with a large group of insecure royals taught me that wealth does not instil self-esteem or self-confidence. The jealousy and infighting among them was quite astonishing. Their competition went as far as pouring billions into businesses heading for bankruptcy. Still they continued to feed those bankrupt businesses in order to save face. They were trapped behind the gate of fear – fear of public shame and humiliation.

They were not only jealous of one another but of my independence and freedom to do as I pleased. If I could have packaged my independence and freedom into a product, they would have bought and paid handsomely for it. Yet feelings of insecurity led the head of the group to weaponize position and money by suddenly terminating my services. I confirmed this was the case ten years later, when I received a call from them – a call to tell me that I was the best consultant they had ever worked with.

Others within the same group weaponized their money by refusing to pay people who had delivered goods and/or services, claiming that they were not up to their standard. How sick do you have to be to abuse people when you know they have earned their money?

USE YOUR POWER OF "NO!"

The power of "No" is the best antidote to such behavior. I make sure that I have the independence, financial freedom and compassion for myself and others to say "No" to abusive customers, friends and colleagues.

A lack of compassion is not just a lack of humanity but a lack of intelligence. Those that lack compassion can barely connect one dot to the next. Compassion and kindness are the highest expressions of what defines our humanity. They bind our communities together. But narrow ethnic and xenophobic identities serve as forces for fear, hatred and destruction. When you connect enough dots in the chain of causality, you discover that mutual gain is the better course of action, leading to the preservation of self-esteem and ultimately human survival.

It takes a high enough level of cognitive and emotional intelligence as well as a healthy ego to comprehend a better alternative than the brutality of fitness rewards for short-term survival. I am not sure that this battle can ever be won. What I do know is that each one of us possesses the power to choose the high road, to walk the path of humanity, instead of the low road of brutality and violence.

COMPASSION IN ACTION

It is no wonder that my Excellence in English Language Teaching competition got a full page in the *Guardian Education Supplement*. A multi-confessional group working together only months after the end of a civil war was news! It was something that "should not happen".

So too was saving the life of a fellow professor by staying locked in my office with a would-be student killer for two hours. It took a while for that student to accept that I would advocate on his behalf. But when I promised to get him the minimum grade he needed, he removed the bullets from his gun.

This is what kindness and compassion can do, to build a better world for humanity to live in.

THE MAGIC OF INTELLIGENT ALTRUISM IS REAL

No matter how hard we try, the cycle between times of relative stability and times of barbarism repeats itself. So what is the truth about the nature of humans? Are we good or bad? Are we both? What has your experience shown you? What have you contributed to – good, bad, both? More importantly, in what direction is your compass for the future pointing?

CHAPTER 11

NO ONE KNOWS THE TRUTH

You have the power to stop the madness by choosing hope over despair. But to avoid taking a lethal dose of something you shouldn't, you need to be able to understand what is in the medicine chest.

NO ONE KNOWS THE TRUTH

What is the truth anyway? We are all hungry for it, yet my experience tells me that no one knows what it is. How can we ever find something when we don't know what we are looking for? Our primal need for "the truth" has fuelled civilization's greatest achievements, greatest errors and greatest atrocities. But even where we have erred, there is a lesson to be salvaged: we can choose which path to take. We have the power to choose construction over destruction.

WE KILL OVER WHOSE TRUTH IS TRUTH

Truth is not fact, and that's why we kill each other over it. We can agree on facts, which are verifiable and objective. Truth is a different matter. The belief that my truth is better than your truth can be fatal. Why? Because if you don't agree, you threaten my fragile identity and my need for certainty. Anything that shakes the foundations upon which identity and certainty are built is seen as an existential threat that must be destroyed.

To avoid the divisions of the truth, we must look to the facts. We can agree on facts, because they are the same for all of us. Without oxygen we die, and with oxygen we live. Developing the habit of looking for the facts is how we can move towards agreement and cooperation.

BEING RIGHT IS EXISTENTIAL AFTER ALL

We do not look for the facts in a vacuum. Our search takes place within an ecosystem of human emotions. These same emotions can derail our search for facts. For example, when fear of rejection or loss of love gets mixed up with our pursuit, we can lose our sense of objectivity and restraint. This is the story of human history: the destruction and reconstruction of civilization after civilization.

From each wave of destruction and reconstruction, ideological and commercial empires emerge. The new version promises better things. We are assured that a superior path has been found: to eternal salvation, to infinite prosperity, to whatever new Mecca is promised us. This is exactly what we want to hear, so we overlook the absence of facts substantiating the new model, willingly accepting the promises we hope to be realized.

Then, inevitably, some way down the line, we discover that it was all just another wishful fantasy spawned by some creative minds.

On the personal level, this perspective of "I am right, and you are wrong" can be just as destructive. The wreckage here is comprised of human relationships. Avoiding such collapses takes the putting aside of emotions, the willingness to look at the facts and the recognition that both parties carry responsibility.

To assume such an attitude is a choice based on trust and hope. It is a choice available to all of us, and one necessary for us all to make if we are ever to progress individually or as a species.

THE GIGANTIC SPIDER'S WEB

Without trust and hope, there is no way forward. When ignorance and the pursuit of convenience combine with our need for love, belonging and certainty, you have the most powerful formula for destruction of all time.

This formula generates a gigantic spider's web of consequences, virtually invisible, irresistible and irreversible, that enmeshes and paralyzes us. And once we are trapped, it is game over. Those beliefs that promised convenience, certainty, love and belonging have delivered none of this, and now it is so much more difficult to take the actions we might have taken.

Can we do better? Can we resist the deadly attraction of the spider's web? As long as we have the ability to make different choices, look for the facts and develop our capabilities, there is great hope.

DIVINE REVELATION OUTPERFORMS COCAINE

We want answers to our questions. We want to satisfy our curiosity. That is why the promise of certainty is so very compelling. We have defined divine revelation as truth and that truth has transformed into belief systems. These belief systems have become integrated into our culture and identity.

Faith in any ideology (religious, political or monetary) and addiction to commercial consumption are exactly the same. Both tap into the fertile soil of ignorance and convenience. That soil is fertilized with the promises of certainty, love and belonging. What a lethal combination, killing independent thinking and enticing us into submission: what we believe in becomes who we are, and what we believe in is submission and compliance.

When culture and identity are threatened by opposing and conflicting beliefs, we unleash wars and other forms of extermination to protect and defend ourselves and destroy our enemies. These destructive actions are based on a win-lose mindset. Destruction is not based on reason or fact or the intelligent management of volatile emotions. Mutual coexistence is rarely, if ever, put forward, as a viable alternative.

The greatest irony is that we do not see any contradiction between such destructive attitudes and the tenets of our belief systems. Most religions espouse virtues of love, advocating that the creations of a god or gods must be protected. Yet our enemies must themselves have been created by the self-same god(s). Taken to their logical (or illogical) conclusions, such belief systems must by necessity accept that good and bad are identical twins; otherwise we have to conclude that for every creator there must be a counter-creator – opposed, antithetical gods.

Factual evidence, unemotional assessment of the situation and critical analysis of the case being presented would go a long way to averting irresponsible decisions and actions. Is this type of higher order thinking possible in the real world? Can we even come close to thinking before reacting on impulse? Can we interrupt the patterns of behavior that result in destructive action, when the temptations to do the opposite are so great?

THE MAGICAL BEANSTALK IS TEMPTING

Religious gurus and prophets, snake oil salespersons and mystical fortune tellers, seers, sexy sirens of the silver screen, the airbrushed influencers of social media – they all have a lot in common. Their promises are always the same: "Here are the seeds of the magic beanstalk, certainty, love and belonging. Take them, please take them, and plant them in the fertile soil of ignorance and convenience. Relax, let go. No effort is required. Just wait and see. They will grow overnight into the magical beanstalk that will take you beyond the clouds. There you can plunder the legendary riches of the giant – he's not human anyway, so it's okay!"

Isn't that the story that repeats from generation to generation, in so many different areas of life?

WHY ARE WE SO FORGETFUL?

So why don't we ever learn? Why do we continue to repeat the same patterns, fall into the same traps, and make the same mistakes over and over? Could it be that we prefer to believe in magic and fairytales? Perhaps it is simply easier than taking responsibility for our lives, easier to follow the promise, "If you follow my version of reality the gates of paradise will be open to you."

But is this all we want for ourselves – to be an economic resource for someone else's benefit? Do we want to be just another in the faceless crowd, a side character in the stories created by others for their own convenience? If your answer to such questions is a resounding 'no!' then there is no substitute for continuous learning, growing and thinking. We have the capacity to walk away; we have the choice of doing what is best for us. But it requires switching off autopilot; it requires consciousness and decision.

Thinking is not an automatic function. Thinking is a learned skill. Thinking is questioning, reflecting and questioning again and again – questions we ask of ourselves and of others. Such questions, such consideration of the answers we receive, informs robust decision making, allowing us to make the right choices.

Are you investing time and effort in developing your thinking and questioning capabilities?

OUR IGNORANCE IS AN ECONOMIC RESOURCE

Pause for a moment and think of the crazy stuff we pay hard earned money for. Holy water, black tulips, magic pills, bone marrow... Butchers used to throw those bones into their garbage bins! Then some food gurus told us that bone marrow has magical properties, and now economic value is generated out of sheer ignorance.

Think about the stuff you pay for and ask, "What am I really trying to buy? Which of these magic beans is most important to me? Love, certainty or belonging?" Then, most importantly, ask yourself if such items will bring what you truly need: personal happiness.

We have the power to change the world by changing our behaviors. And to change our behavior, we must first change our thoughts. Our thoughts lead to feelings and our feelings lead to our actions; the sum of our actions are our behaviors. If we do not like the results of our behaviours, we must go back to square one. What were you thinking?

SPIRITUALITY IS A DIMENSION NOT YET UNDERSTOOD

Some would say we are a complex physical, electrical and chemical manifestation. But the heart of the matter is that we are an intricate combination of body, mind, emotions and spirit. We can by no means dismiss spirituality as a dimension of human existence. We do not fully understand, and may never understand, what comprises the human mind. Whether we think of it as consciousness or life force, it is very hard to study ourselves by ourselves.

This humble admission of ignorance can keep us in check. By admitting that we really don't know what we are, we can maintain a curious and open mind and remain capable of growth. Learning, growing and making better decisions and more informed choices is how we evolve. When we stop evolving towards the best version of ourselves, we lose the very essence of our humanity. Our curiosity is the flame that powers our desire for continual learning and growth. We must keep that flame aglow.

WE LUST FOR THE TRUTH

Because we are all hungry for the truth, those promising to share it with us can prove irresistible. Have you ever wondered why the words "secret", "reveal", "mystery", "free", "easy" and on and on are so attractive? And have you noticed how frequently these words are used in advertising?

But in the persuasion business, the mother and father of all bombs is sex. We want protectors, connectors, lovers and invincible forces to keep us safe. This is how marketing hooks us; this is how religions and ideologies take root.

Sex is the ultimate reward in many religions. If you take the time to read some holy books, you will discover that many passages read like pornography. You will also notice that others read like masterful advertising copy.

CONVENIENCE IS A MAGIC PILL

Those of us looking for the truth have many unanswered and inconvenient questions, and we must labor for our answers. Yet those looking for convenience will find it everywhere. The latest and greatest elixirs, panaceas and magic pills will be thrust into their hands.

We have accomplished the unthinkable, looking billions of lightyears into galaxies far beyond the Milky Way. We have enough food to feed the world. We have spare parts when our organs fail. We are remarkable creatures when we choose to be, and yet we do not always choose to be remarkable.

What we look for sets the compass. If you look for love and belonging, you will find creams and potions, hair dyes and extensions, botox, implants and fillers. But if you look for self-fulfilment and happiness you will need to start at the source.

That source is knowing who you are and who you are meant to be. Regardless of your inclination, there is one path on which we all meet.

DON'T CONFUSE PLEASURE WITH HAPPINESS

Too many of us are looking for what humanity has always looked for: to gain pleasure and to avoid pain. Pleasure is pure dopamine, fast and effective, but the effect fades as quickly as it came. Happiness is dopamine plus serotonin. This combination doesn't fade fast; it offers a sense of inner wellbeing. Dopamine can be addictive because we need regular shots to keep us feeling good. Serotonin does the opposite; it keeps us feeling serene, relaxed and happy.

The substitution of pleasure for happiness has earned billions for many industries. It is the ultimate gold mine.

INSECURE LEADERSHIP IS A DISASTER WAITING TO HAPPEN

Regardless of color or creed, the types of leaders who promise pleasure and protection from pain are very dangerous. This promise is the oxymoron of all time: "I am both your protector and your predator. I alone can protect you because I have the power of predation."

People like Charles Manson are able to march people off to willing suicide, not only of themselves but of their children. The deadly attraction Manson offered was protection and predation in one package.

This is exactly the same dynamic that occurs in abusive relationships, exploitative businesses, schools and universities, dictatorships actual or disguised. We live in a jungle full of predators, and we must build the strength and the skills necessary to prevail against them.

At times, it may seem as if we have no way to resist, but that's incorrect. We always have the power to choose. We lose only when we forget this. We have the power to accept or reject concepts, think our own thoughts, choose how we behave, how we influence the lives of others, whether or not we learn, grow or give up and thousands of other pathways.

At every junction of our life's journey, we can decide on the direction we want to take. We have the power if only we choose to use it.

THE HAND THAT ROCKS THE CRADLE HAS POWER

Our ancestors managed to survive their own jungles, to pass on their genetic code to us. We must keep in mind the qualities and knowledge of our forebearers', not least the cliché "the hand that rocks the cradle, rocks the world". If you can't afford to educate your daughter and your son at the same time, educate your daughter first. She is the one who will more directly shape the future of the next generation.

This is not to say that you should neglect your sons. Both women and men need to be senior partners as they journey through life together. Those who raise healthy, balanced, thinking humans hold the power to change the world. I can't say it enough times: the greatest gifts we can give our children are solid self-esteem and high self-confidence. This is how we immunize them against the toxic spider's web. There is no job on earth that is more important than preparing the next generation to face the sirens that entice them in the direction of the rocks that will destroy them.

This ability to learn every day, think critically, problem solve, stand up for themselves and approach the future with optimism will furnish them with the resilience, foresight and the adaptability to find a better way.

LOOK AT THE FACTS AND THE IMPLICATIONS

The truth is not fact. We have defined divine revelation as truth and that truth has been transformed into belief systems. These belief systems have become integrated into our model of the world. But have they helped make the world a better place?

If we have any doubts that the world has become antithetical to human survival and wellbeing, here are a few facts to consider.

Birth rates worldwide are dropping dramatically. This is particularly apparent in developed countries where birth rates are as low as or even lower than 0.5%. Housing costs in the developed world are such that most young people will never be able to purchase a home.

Global productivity by country has been declining since the 1970s. Education has been diluted, degrading our previous definitions of adult literacy. Military spending is ten times higher than education spending in the U.S.A.

The divide between rich and poor is huge and continues to grow. 1% of Americans have enough money to buy 99% of US homes. The average one-percenter has 600 times more than the average citizen.

YOU CAN DO SOMETHING ABOUT IT.

You are the one who must chart a rational pathway out of this. You must equip yourself with the knowledge, skills and capabilities that broaden the range of choices you can make. We can and must do better than this.

Be inspired by the astounding things we have achieved as a species. Step away from the precipice of hatred and destruction. Close your ears to the tune of the Pied Piper. Learn, develop and grow.

We may not have the power to change geopolitical policy or overcome media manipulation, the dumbing down of education and the mass drugging of societies. But we do have the power to do something about our own lives. We do not have to buy into the madness. As long as we have the power to decide where *we* want to go, to make considered choices and decisions, we have an exit strategy. We can survive and thrive even under such conditions.

CHAPTER 12

LEADERS FOR ALL SEASONS PUT THEMSELVES FIRST

It is not selfish to put yourself first. In fact, it is your greatest responsibility to do so. Those who don't, give up a significant part of what makes us human.

TAKE YOURSELF SERIOUSLY AND SO WILL OTHERS

You must put yourself first to earn the position of leader and maintain it through all the seasons of your life. A leader is a person who has the ability to influence others for better or for worse. I am talking about positive influence, the kind of influence that encourages and motivates others because it sets a standard they aspire to reach.

Putting yourself first means taking the responsibility to become and continue to become the best version of yourself possible.

BLAME TAKES YOU DOWN A DEAD END

We know that we have the power to change ourselves, but all too often we do not act on that knowledge. Instead, we keep looking outside of ourselves for people to blame and find fault with. This makes us feel superior but all we are doing is projecting the things we don't like about ourselves onto others.

The attraction of quick fixes is compelling, because of the enticing promise of success without effort. At some level we know that this is not possible, but the temptation is such that we often fall into the trap.

But there is a better and more practical path to the improvement of the human condition. There is so much you can do to realize your full potential. You really don't have the time to find fault with others. Take the path to self-fulfilment and happiness.

IT ISN'T COMPLICATED, IT ONLY REQUIRES A DECISION.

To make our lives fulfilling is not complicated; it only takes the time to understand, plan and apply. We need to develop and grow in four major areas: the mental, the physical, the emotional and the spiritual. The purpose of our lives is to become better in every way, and to facilitate further improvement in the next generation. Becoming better requires focus on the priorities of growth and development. To do so, we must resist the temptations of quick fixes, the diversions of magical solutions and the fiction of success without effort.

WHAT'S YOUR ROLE ON THE CHESSBOARD?

These interruptions and temptations are ever present. Our lives are not easy. We have responsibilities and obligations to meet and many obstacles to overcome as we go about the necessities of life. Survival activities leave little time for us to stop and think. As a result, we become dependent and compliant, inculcating this obedience generation after generation. How can we break this destructive cycle? What do we do?

The first step is to answer two basic questions: "Why are we here?" and "Where are we going?" The aim is not to determine the ultimate goal of human existence but to understand our individual purpose. Is our goal to live, reproduce and then to die? Is that all it is?

The answer is "yes" for the large majority. That's it! But leaders do not see it that way. Whether rightly or wrongly, they want more from their lives. They ask themselves difficult questions and try to make sense of the world. These people are a minority. If you are in that minority, it is because you ask uncomfortable questions.

LIVE OR KILL?

Is the goal of humanity peace, prosperity, sustainable growth and cooperation? Or is the goal war, destruction, exploitation and subjugation? The former gives us hope and the latter mutually assured destruction. Let's assume for a moment that we achieve the level of enlightenment and wisdom that enables us to redefine the role of governments and the role of humanity. That we realize that the true purpose of humanity is to achieve its full potential in all dimensions of human development. What's stopping you from achieving that as an individual or as a family?

We aren't helpless, as long as we can decide and choose to follow our unique path.

DO YOU KNOW YOUR USP?

What is your USP (unique selling point) as a human being? What are you supposed to do with your superior intelligence and capabilities? Surely you are going to treat yourself better than you treat a high-tech piece of equipment. Most of us use our advanced equipment for a few basic purposes. We may never read the manual or explore the full range of possibilities it offers. We may never know what the equipment could have done for us before it breaks down and has to be discarded. But we should treat ourselves better. We should do whatever it takes to realize our full potential as far as possible.

THINKING IS CENTRAL

Let's begin with mental development. We know so much that we do not apply in the service of achieving our human potential. Thinking is a learned process. Learning to think critically and analytically is the foundation of clear thinking. Clear thinking is the foundation of clear communication. Clear communication is the foundation of understanding and connecting with others.

Developing the skills of scientific thinking versus magical

thinking is the responsibility of every individual person, parent and educator.

PARENTS NEED UPDATING

Unfortunately, we aren't born with an operations manual that tells us how to optimize our brains. Parents and others responsible for the growth and development of the next generation need more support. Developmental psychology and practical parenting skills must be taught methodically, offered as part of the educational program. An effective parental education program should accompany and run in parallel with the school curriculum. The educational program must be updated and expanded regularly as we learn more about how to develop informed and well-adjusted societies.

NOTHING IS ALL BLACK OR ALL WHITE

In the times when my husband was calm and caring, our children got the benefit of both parents' capabilities. We engaged them with challenging questions and discussions, encouraged close observation of what was going on around them and tried to help them make sense of it. Spotting logical fallacies, the process of distinguishing fact from opinion, was part of casual conversations, chess and similar games of strategy a part of our routine. Learning was an adventure driven by curiosity and discovery. It gives me hope and pleasure when I see my children raising their children in the same way.

GROWTH IS PERPETUAL

The journey of growth continues throughout life. Acquiring new knowledge, skills and capabilities is a matter of course. I see this in the lives of my children and grandchildren, so I know that it can be done. Writing, presenting, conversing, listening and interacting with others – this is what it means to be human; this is what continuous development entails.

Without continuous learning, critical thinking and freedom of expression, the future of the next generation is mental enslavement. When we can't think for ourselves, we become hostages to a closed system of circular thinking, where fear of loss stultifies our mind.

Engage in conversations that seek to understand through questioning and listening. Expand your model of the world with the help of your insatiable curiosity. Socrates developed this method of teaching and learning 2,500 years ago. It has proven its worth, so why wouldn't we use it on a regular basis?

NO SUBSTITUTE FOR GOOD HEALTH

Physical wellbeing is another foundational pillar of realizing our full potential. Physical wellbeing starts at conception and should be a lifelong pursuit. Is it time to take a critical look at what we teach in schools and universities? There is no excuse for omitting the priorities necessary for healthy lives and healthy societies. We should not make ourselves hosts for pharmaceutical companies. A dog with too many ticks will die, and when the host dies, the parasites also die.

I had the good fortune to go to a school where education was highly valued and where the purpose of that education was to produce well-rounded humans. Our education was designed to enable us to manage our lives even if we never went to university. Two of the subjects we studied that I find extremely valuable to this day were Health Science and Cookery (Nutrition and Home Economics). These subjects ran across three or four years. Each year introduced a new dimension.

We learned about communicable and non-communicable diseases, parasites, hygiene and much, much more. We learned the foundation of human nutrition, the importance of balanced meals and how to design and cook them. We learned how to prepare meals for infants and diabetics and how to conserve vitamins and minerals through appropriate cooking methods and temperatures.

TOO GOOD TO LAST

Unfortunately, my children didn't have the opportunity to go to such a school. By the time they were school age, examination scores and school ratings had become the most important aspects of "education". The not-for-profit model had morphed into something that looked more like a corporate business. Nevertheless, I passed on my knowledge and skills to my children, and they took it upon themselves to take their own knowledge and skills many levels higher. They are now passing these on to their children and friends.

There are many forward-looking schools with exciting curricula, but they are in a minority. Where formal education fails us, we must take up the mantle.

THERE IS ALWAYS A BRIGHT SIDE

Life always presents us with challenges and with every challenge comes enormous opportunities. When we were trapped at home because of the war, doing things together in the kitchen kept me and my children sane.

We made up weekly menus and all participated in turning them into meals on the table. And when it was safe to go out, we went on hikes and picnics. My children still enjoy outdoor adventures with their families. Maintaining physical wellbeing through good nutrition and exercise is a matter of lifestyle. When healthy activities become habits, we enjoy a healthy lifestyle, which we can then pass on to the next generation.

Physical wellbeing contributes to personal, social and global stability. For one thing, it significantly lowers the burden of national healthcare budgets. Pharmaceutical and insurance companies may not welcome such a prospect, but they too would benefit from it. If healthcare provision were to become *real* healthcare, as opposed to sick care, which it is at present, we could all enjoy so many innovative products and services for regular daily use. Their customers would be everybody, not just sick bodies.

PARENTING IS THE LYNCHPIN

When we understand the difference between education and brainwashing, we can promote good nutrition and exercise instead of unnecessary pills and potions. We owe it to ourselves and those we care about to understand what constitutes healthy food.

Education starts at home. We must read and understand the labels of food items. We must inform ourselves about safe agricultural practices. Once we are equipped with such knowledge, we can improve our wider societies, demanding of our governments better oversight, driven by science and not short-term, illicit gains.

Ignorance is an enormous economic resource to the unscrupulous and predatory greed of the marketers. We can't hold anyone accountable if we are uninformed, unable to think critically or ask uncomfortable questions and demand answers.

THERE IS NO SUBSTITUTE FOR EMOTIONAL INTELLIGENCE

Emotional wellbeing is the foundation of a healthy relationship with ourselves and others. But what does it mean? Self-awareness is the first building block and must be continuously deepened as we go from infancy to adulthood. Children are far more intelligent than we give them credit for, and we need to remind ourselves to treat them with respect.

Emotional intelligence is about becoming aware of what we are thinking about or focussing on and the feelings that such focus and thoughts generate. We need to learn how to manage this awareness in positive and responsible ways. Learning to respect the feelings and emotions of others is a start. We need to help both others and ourselves understand the source of our feelings. With this understanding, we can respond appropriately. It is within everyone's reach to do so.

ARDUOUS BUT RICHLY REWARDING

It is a long and arduous journey, progressing from mindless reaction to thoughtful response. But imagine how different the world would be if only we could develop this capability during our childhoods and continue to hone and perfect it throughout our lives. The world would be a much better place if it was peopled by humans who behaved like humans – humans conscious, self-aware, and able to manage themselves and relate to others in a healthy and constructive manner!

Such self-mastery is the path to self-esteem and self-confidence, the antidote to self-loathing, fear and hatred. The better adjusted we are, the easier it is to diffuse hostile emotions towards those whom we mistakenly believe are responsible for our dissatisfactions. Low self-esteem and low self-awareness result in people with sick egos – abusive parents, CEOs, world leaders, teachers and bullies. All of the above suffer from the same root cause. All of the above are responsible for millions of wrecked lives, deaths and misery.

SOUL OR SPIRIT – YOU MUST HAVE ONE

The fourth of the pillars of balanced human development is the spiritual dimension. I am not talking about religion. I am talking about our capacity to use our imagination to bring into existence things that did not exist before. If you are breathing, you must have a soul or a spirit. It expresses itself through your creative imagination. This capacity is powerful, capable of constructive or destructive outputs and outcomes.

We all possess a greater or smaller capacity for imagination.

However, depending on our mental and physical health, the results can be monstrous or divine. It is like launching a rocket to the moon. If the trajectory is even slightly off, the divergence becomes amplified as the journey progresses, and we miss the target entirely.

HEAVEN AND HELL ARE MAN MADE

Our ability to use our capabilities for positive and creative purposes is awe inspiring. Art, music, science, technology, engineering, medicine and many more disciplines – they are all expressions of our uniquely human spirits.

Our ability to use our capabilities for negative and creative purposes is also awe inspiring. Deforestation, mining, bombing, poisoning, polluting, killing – these are all expressions of the sickness in our souls.

The value we give to ourselves is the value we assign to our environment and our fellow humans. What is your vibrational signature and what is the nature of the vibrations you transmit?

It is a question to ask every day, as we look into the mirror of our life. As we move forward from the alpha to the omega of our lives, what is the legacy we leave behind us, one closer to heaven or to hell?

What have you done today that moves the world to a better place? Whom have you thanked or recognized in some way? With what new capabilities have you enriched yourself? What kindness and compassion have you shown to a fellow human? Have you looked in the mirror and made some non-surgical, personal improvements?

ABOUT THE AUTHOR

A former dean with fifty years of academic and business experience, Fay is an international, award-winning, change management strategist. The founder and CEO of ICTN, she coaches, consults and trains leading multinationals globally.

Fay has established schools, universities and four businesses. She has delivered thousands of experiential workshops to public and private sectors and published 500 articles on business culture and leadership.

As a Strategic Intervention & Leadership Coach, Fay works with leaders, CEOs, board members, presidents and ministers of government to meet the challenges of change within their organizations.

As a Culture Transformation Consultant, Fay applies her expertise in advanced psychometrics, hypnotherapy and neuroscience to design and deliver bespoke programs. Fay focuses on Leadership, Strategic Communication and Business Emotional Intelligence.

"The Four Journeys of a Leader"© is Fay's flagship leadership development program.

Her family consists of recognized scientists, engineers, artists, authors, inventors, grand-parents and eight talented grandchildren